CONTEMPORARY
VOCATIONAL REHABILITATION

This is the third volume of a program of books dealing with rehabilitation literature published by New York University Press.

1. Vocational Rehabilitation of the Disabled: An Overview by David Malikin and Herbert Rusalem, 1968.

2. Social Disability by David Malikin, 1973.

3. Contemporary Vocational Rehabilitation by Herbert Rusalem and David Malikin, 1976.

CONTEMPORARY
VOCATIONAL REHABILITATION

Edited by
HERBERT RUSALEM

Teachers College
Columbia University

DAVID MALIKIN

New York University

New York: NEW YORK UNIVERSITY PRESS · 1976

200078

Library of Congress Catalog Card Number: 75-7523
ISBN: 0-8147-5403-1

Library of Congress Cataloging in Publication Data
Main entry under title:

Contemporary vocational rehabilitation.

   Includes bibliographies.
   1. Vocational rehabilitation—Addresses, essays,
lectures. I. Rusalem, Herbert. II. Malikin,
David, 1913-
HD7255.C65   362.8′5   75-7523
ISBN 0-8147-5403-1

Manfactured in the United States of America

PREFACE

When the first volume in this series—Vocational Rehabilitation of the Disabled: An Overview—was published in 1968, the editors and publisher had modest estimations of its potential impact. As time passed, sales exceeded expectations and professors, students, administrators and practitioners responded favorably to the book. Thus, it became increasingly clear that the text was filling a need for an overall introduction to the field of vocational rehabilitation. In 1974, when the New York University Press had substantially depleted its available copies of the book, the question was raised concerning a revision of the original volume to bring it up to date with current developments in vocational rehabilitation. At that time, since the first book retained much relevance, despite its age, it was felt that it could serve as the basis for a continuing series which could periodically bring the textual materials up to date and approach the subject matter in a somewhat different way.

The present book differs from the earlier one by departing from the largely factual and reportorial approach that characterized its predecessor. Instead, the new book addresses itself more consciously to controversial topics and ideas with the chapter authors being encouraged to express their own opinions, regardless of their deviance from conventional thought. The result is a more vibrant and challenging book that is more likely to arouse feelings. In view of the perils that now confront vocational rehabilitation, a more controversial presentation may be in order to generate improved planning. More than ever, we desperately need new perspectives and solutions if our field is to survive. Fewer authors have participated in the preparation of the chapters in this book than in the earlier one because not all the leaders in our field are comfortable with controversy or ready to deal with the consequences of frank statements of opinion about sensitive areas. Thus, the contributors to this volume are not only thoughtful writers about the state of vocational rehabilitation, but they are also prepared to interact with the feedback and dissonance that is likely to be engendered by offbeat ideas.

The editors have provided brief introductions and follow-ups to all the chapters in an effort to orient readers to the context in which the chapter's subject is being discussed and to help them to consider some of the implications for vocational rehabilitation. The central idea of the chapters and the accompanying explicative material is to help readers think a problem through without imposing a fixed position upon them. Although the chapter authors are authorities in their fields, they are the first to concede that their positions are tentative and subject to change as verifying or contradictory information becomes available. If vocational rehabilitation is to weather the hazards of limited funding, mismanagement, inappropriate service delivery systems, and dehumanization, all of us will have to think through the issues that face us more carefully and imaginatively. If this book broadens readers' horizons and enables them to arrive at more effective and creative solutions to current vocational rehabilitation problems, it will have fulfilled its central objective.

The editors are grateful to the chapter authors for their contributions and to the New York University Press staff for its helpfulness and patience. The editors also wish to acknowledge the perceptiveness and sophistication of the professors, students, practitioners, and administrators who have given us astute response about the first book. Many of the changes that appear in the format of the current volume were derived from their suggestions and ideas. Finally, the editors wish to thank their respective wives, Rae Malikin and Helen Rusalem for their understanding and assistance during the difficult days when the manuscripts was being prepared.

Herbert Rusalem, Ed. D.
David Malikin, Ph. D.

CONTRIBUTORS

Celia Benney, Associate Executive Director, Altro Health and Rehabilitation Services, Inc., New York City

David Malikin, Professor of Rehabilitation Counseling, New York University, New York City

Walter S. Neff, Professor of Psychology, New York University, New York City

Samuel H. Osipow, Professor and Chairman, Department of Psychology, Ohio State University, Columbus, Ohio

Lila Rosenblum, Coordinator, Speech and Hearing Counseling Service, ICD Rehabilitation and Research Center, New York City

Herbert Rusalem, Professor of Special Education, Teachers College, Columbia University, New York City

Jerome Siller, Professor of Educational Psychology, New York University, New York City

Daniel Sinick, Professor of Education, Director, Rehabilitation Counselor Education, George Washington University, Washington, D.C.

Frederick A. Whitehouse, Professor of Rehabilitation, Director, Rehabilitation Counselor Training Program, Hofstra University, Hempstead, New York

Contents

PART I:

THE CURRENT REHABILITATION SCENE

CHAPTER I

ISSUES IN REHABILITATION

SETTING THE SCENE

Webster defines an issue as "an outflow, a means of going out, a point, matter or question to be disputed or decided, a sending or giving out, to be born." In essence, an issue appears when different views are offered for discussion so that ultimately some resolution may be reached for the benefit of all. That is the purpose of this chapter: to identify seven current major issues of concern to rehabilitation, to stimulate discussion about them by delineating their parameters, and to encourage workers in the field to examine their positions, and to participate in the problem resolution process.

In choosing to deal with the issues of theory, service delivery systems, research use, administrative styles, the survival of voluntary agencies, the vocational component, and favored and unfavored disability groups, it is not inferred that these are necessarily the only, or even the most urgent, unfinished business facing the rehabilitation field today. However, they are some of the important issues that merit attention, and, rather than argue about their primacy, it might be more useful for readers to jump in and grapple with each of the selected issues.

The rehabilitation literature is filled with descriptions of service programs, reports of research findings, information about upcoming organizational events and the outcomes of such meetings, but rarely do we deal with the real "gut" issues of our time. To argue or disagree is to expose oneself to counterforces. Thus, it is much safer for some of us to avoid disputation. However, the dialectic process applies as much to the arena of ideas as it does to physical matter, and it is only from the clash of antithetical thinking that new and more valid insights emerge. Perhaps you would like to come to grips with these open rehabilitation issues of our time.

CHAPTER I

ISSUES IN REHABILITATION

HERBERT RUSALEM

In its more than 50 years of service to the American people, the formal rehabilitation movement has faced and resolved an endless series of critical issues. In just the past few decades, a proliferation of controversies have been settled and the decisions emerging therefrom have become integral everyday components in rehabilitation practice. For example:

- Virtually no one still questions the responsibility of rehabilitation agencies for working with mentally retarded, emotionally disabled, homebound, institutionalized, or other severely handicapped individuals.
- Virtually no one doubts the proposition that social-psychological variables play a major role in determining rehabilitation success and that rehabilitation programs, therefore, should incorporate sophisticated behavioral interventions.
- Virtually no one still holds that most rehabilitation clients can be assisted merely through counseling. On the contrary, environmental components have become so important that there has been a vast expansion of rehabilitation facilities of many types, all of which use a planned and structured milieu as a major rehabilitation tool.
- Relatively few diehards still raise the question as to whether rehabilitation counseling is merely an arm of social work and that the social casework approach holds the greater promise of rehabilitating the greatest number of vocational rehabilitation clients.
- Only a handful of hard-liners still feel that the client's place is

7

solely in the hands of the rehabilitation worker. Increasingly, the client's role in fashioning his own rehabilitation, as well as the rehabilitation of others, is becoming an integral aspect of rehabilitation practice.

Just these few instances suggest that the rehabilitation movement, as a resilient and flexible response to changing conditions and caseloads has had the capacity to raise, cope with, and resolve critical issues. In all fairness, it must be admitted that these resolutions did not always come about without resistance, delays, and bitterness but may be expected in any field when new questions suggest new answers that are not entirely acceptable to old practitioners. The important thing, however, is that even after the stormiest of controversies, rehabilitation issues generally have been "cooled" and, as the turbulence surrounding them have subsided, the agreements reached became incorporated into the prevailing federal-state voluntary agency rehabilitation program.

Today, as in the past, there is no dearth of rehabilitation issues. Indeed, virtually every rehabilitation worker and client is ready to specify his or her concerns and suggest solutions. People in state rehabilitation agencies are understandably concerned with current funding conditions, local agencies are perplexed by the vagaries of state rehabilitation and prepaid medical plan fees, individual counselors chafe under heavy and difficult caseloads, rehabilitation supervisors complain about the quality and the training of rehabilitation workers, voluntary agencies are anxious about possible state agency authoritarian attitudes toward them, and rehabilitation clients sometimes feel short-changed by a system that, in practice, too often focuses upon a first job rather than a long-term career that will be congruent with their potentialities. These and many other critical rehabilitation issues are in the forefront of current thinking in the field. They are discussed privately, in rehabilitation offices, at conferences, at in-service training sessions, in college classrooms, and wherever people interested in rehabilitation congregate. Each of these issues merits extensive consideration and were it not for space limitations, should be discussed in this chapter. At the risk of turning off some readers, however, this material will focus upon other and, perhaps, more global issues.

Rehabilitation is a highly pragmatic and down-to-earth field. Dealing everyday, with practical and compelling human problems, rehabilitation workers rarely have the luxury of stepping back and viewing their field with a long-range perspective. Occasionally, special task forces or committees, often related to planning efforts, have examined critical underlying issues in depth, but, in all too many cases, the convergent thinking of the task force participants and the consensus orientation of these groups have resulted in rather conventional restatements of already rehashed questions. In the belief that the time has arrived for some other questions to be spotlighted, this chapter will attempt to pierce the underbelly of rehabilitation and hopefully, come forth with a few basic and far-reaching issues that warrant extensive discussion and ultimate resolution.

Does Rehabilitation Need a Theory?

The word theory connotes an overarching explanation of a wide variety of related phenomena. A theory improves predictive precision, suggests lines of research, provides an overall framework for planning, and indicates directions for present or future development. In practical terms, it enables a field to organize itself rationally and systematically so that those who participate in it share a common frame of reference in their attempts to cope with short- and long-range human problems. To a certain extent, rehabilitation has already adopted certain far-reaching ideas which could serve as precursors to a full-fledged theory or an incorporated one. Among these may be the concepts of rehabilitation potential, the regenerative influence of employment, and the durability of the human drive for attainment and acceptance. These are, indeed, valuable components for a possible rehabilitation theory, but they have not yet been conceptualized in terms that constitute a comprehensive theoretical formulation.

An issue in this area arises because some rehabilitation practitioners do not feel a need for a theory. They operate on a day-to-day basis, handling situations as they occur on a common sense or intuitive basis. As they see it, each challenge is to be met on its own terms in a manner which best fits current conditions without reference to any abiding frame of reference or guideposts. On the other hand, some rehabilitation workers feel a need for a philosophical substructure that is so consistently correct in predicting and explaining rehabilitation phenomena that it gives meaning, precision, direction, and greater probability of success to everyday rehabilitation practice. At the moment

relatively few rehabilitation workers are pressing for the fuller development and adoption of a rehabilitation theory. Yet, the lack of a
viable theory may have contributed to a number of rehabilitation
disappointments that occurred in the late 1960s and early 1970s, such
as presidential vetoes of rehabilitation legislation, funding difficulties,
the modest success with culturally disadvantaged clients, and the en-
trenchment of bureaucrats rather than rehabilitators in leadership
positions in a number of agencies.

Most leaders and practitioners have implicit theories about rehabilitation. In many instances, these personal theories are incompatible
or inconsistent with each other, suggesting the need for a synthesizing
effort that welds these diverse notions into a single comprehensive
concept. This author believes that future theory-building in this field,
if it occurs at all, will gradually cluster around learning capacities.
Since all rehabilitation activities require disabled persons to learn
new responses, everything in the rehabilitation movement may fall
into place in a type of learning theory which explains equally well why
clients do or do not learn rehabilitation tasks, why rehabilitation workers do or do not learn to adapt to changing conditions, and why many
rehabilitation administrators fail to meet their responsibility for shaping and implementing new movements. Even if the learning capacities
concept proves unacceptable as a fulcrum for theory-building other
concepts have promise, but their value will not be known until the
need for a rehabilitation theory is established and various cores for
such a theory are explored.

Is the Present Vocational Rehabilitation Service Delivery System the Most Favorable One That Can Be Devised?

The vocational rehabilitation service delivery system first developed
in the 1920s has been expanded and extended almost immeasurably,
particularly in terms of the number of agencies, programs, personnel,
and clients served, and the quality of the programs offered. In addition,
innovative service delivery approaches have been grafted onto the
system with gratifying regularity, including special provisions for
working with schools, colleges, hospitals, voluntary agencies, outreach
stations, state employment services, social security, housing groups,
consumer organizations, institutions and residences, community-wide

comprehensive service programs, labor unions, business and industry, and health organizations. The soundness of the original vocational rehabilitation service delivery concept is suggested by the high degree of success achieved in splicing each new ramification into the system. Indeed, no other human service delivery system has incorporated so many alterations and additions without vitiating the essential character and strength of its total design.

Despite this, recommendations are periodically made for a major overhaul of the total effort. Such recommendations do not ignore the outstanding service record and hardiness of the existing system, but note is taken of the fact that even today only a minority of those who conceivably could benefit from rehabilitation services are receiving them; that the less disabled receive a disproportionately high incidence of service while the most disabled are less adequately provided for; that recent setbacks in funding, political and public support, and bureaucratic infighting in some areas suggest weaknesses in the system. These alleged evidences of decline are cited as symptoms of organizational and programmatic arteriosclerosis, reflecting a less vigorous, powerful, and dynamic service establishment. Some would argue this is a consequence of the original service delivery concept being pushed beyond its limits of accommodation and that the system is coming apart at its structural seams. On the other hand, large numbers of rehabilitation workers give little credence to this position and hold to the view that there is life in the "old girl" yet and that we haven't begun to approach the outer limits of possible accommodation in the existing service delivery model. Whatever the merits of calls for change, some rehabilitation workers cannot conceive of a replacement for the prevailing model, declaring that a departure from it now could well precipitate a dismantling of the generally commendable programs we now have.

The mounting problems of the rehabilitation movement in the 1970s suggest that the vortex of this service delivery question is likely to engulf the field in the next few years. During the Nixon Administration, some officials gave consideration to a voucher system under which clients would purchase their own rehabilitation services without the major intervention of a professional state vocational rehabilitation service. In some instances, it has been hypothesized that rehabilitation counseling need not be at the center of the rehabilitation process and that medical, psychotherapeutic, or social service modes could serve as well or better. During the next few years, a crossroads is likely to be reached at which a total reexamination will be made of the very foundations of the current system, including a consideration of alternative service delivery models. It is difficult to say whether out of this review still another "band-aid" will be applied to the still intact original vocational rehabilitation service delivery system or whether an entirely different system will emerge for bringing more disabled persons into a more meaningful relationship with rehabilitation services.

Can the Present Gap That Exists Between the Generation of Rehabilitation Research Findings and Their Application to Service Problems Be Closed to a Significant Degree?

Research utilization is as slow a process in rehabilitation as it is in other behavioral science fields. However, in view of rehabilitation's responsibility for the future development of millions of disabled Americans the customary ten to fifteen years of research utilization delay seems intolerable. In rehabilitation offices and facilities throughout the United States, disabled persons are working with rehabilitation personnel toward the solution of critical life problems using outmoded tools. Vital and relevant research findings already exist that would facilitate the attainment of rehabilitation goals, but much of this knowledge is either unknown to or unaccepted by the clinicians. Indeed, there are rehabilitation workers who deny that behavioral science research can produce anything of value for the disabled. As these individuals assess the output of the rehabilitation research enterprise, they find much that is impractical, theoretical, and academic. For them, rehabilitation progress and development will come about, as it has in the past, through unceasing day-to-day experience and hardheaded field work in solving problems for disabled individuals. For them, the issue is not research utilization but the question as to whether the funds spent on research might not better be spent on additional service.

Another issue arises, however, among rehabilitation workers who accept research as a vital necessity but who cannot gain ready access to its products. A variety of utilization techniques have been devised for their benefit, including publications in the professional literature, reports at professional conferences, research briefs, change agents, legislative and political action, and persuasion and education. Each of these procedures has had its successes but none has yet succeeded in reducing substantially the lag between research findings and everyday rehabilitation practice. Less noticed in attempts to deal with this issue are innovative utilization methods borrowed from other fields or home-brewed by rehabilitation researchers. For example, the Programmatic Research Project on the Rehabilitation of Homebound Persons (Rusalem, 1975) yielded unequivocal data indicating that there is a vast vocational rehabilitation potential in homebound persons. Yet, these findings did not readily enter rehabilitation practice until the project found, indoctrinated, and supported the trend-setting utilization efforts of local community leaders who were interested in this client group and became volunteer affiliates of the project. Targeted local leadership combined with research support enabled more than 25 communities to overcome local apathy, inaction, and resistance so that the first steps toward developing homebound rehabilitation programming could be taken.

The central issue in this area that is emerging centers around the current general incapacity of rehabilitation practitioners and researchers, alone or in tandem, to expedite early application of research findings to client's problems. In the course of the resolution of this issue, decisions will have to be made whether to entrust this vital function to practitioners, researchers, or both, or to a new breed of rehabilitation worker concerned primarily with research utilization. Until issues of this type are resolved, lives that could be more readily restored through new but little-used knowledge will continue to be wasted while vital data gathers dust on library shelves.

Should the Rehabilitation Movement Be Led by Professional Administrators Who Are Committed to Organizational Efficiency and Rationality, Rather Than Creativity?

Rehabilitation's pioneers often were idiosyncratic "naturals" who operated as the "Edisons" of their field. With relatively little specialized training and virtually no scientific back-up, they pursued their inner visions with courage and tenacity. The products of their efforts are evident in much of what rehabilitation is today. Along the way, however, rehabilitation agencies and facilities grew in size and complexity. When these early leaders found themselves administering large establishments that were quite remote from the personalized organizations that they had headed only a few years earlier, they were ill-prepared for the challenge. Not only were they uncomfortable in these new settings, but it soon became evident that the day-to-day demands of conducting large-scale programs required other types of abilities. Gradually, professional administrators penetrated rehabilitation in both the public and the private sectors. When this occurred, it became immediately obvious that they had the tidy, well-organized, detail-grasping minds needed to perform many of the administrative functions of rehabilitation agencies, such as budgeting, internal controls, systems analysis, cost accounting, personnel administrations, fiscal frugality, accountability, and precise scheduling.

The rise of the professional administrator brought order out of chaos for many a rehabilitation agency, keeping it afloat and financially secure. But other changes came with this new type of administrator. One can recall the informal, ad hoc, and personalized atmosphere of certain national and state rehabilitation agencies in earlier decades. They were inefficient and unsystematic, perhaps, but they had this in common: If a client required a creative plan, an ingenious arrangement, or a program that fell outside the usual parameters, that client obtained what he or she needed. And, it was fun to work for those organizations since administrators could cut corners, be friends with their staffs, and take risks without fear of being investigated at every turn. Today, rehabilitation agencies in most communities are more formal organized enterprises in which the game is played according to the book.

Even more noticeable is the phenomenon of current administrators, trained in orderly management processes, being unable to perceive their function in human terms. Recently, I attended a high-level professional workshop in the Middle West that had been assigned the task of evolving a curriculum for deaf-blind teenagers. The director of the workshop was a distinguished systems management specialist who could not be deterred from following his preconceived system in conducting this workshop. His preoccupation with the preplanned structure of this mission relegated deaf-blind youth to the status of an abstraction subsidiary in importance to the carefully worked out system which was imposed upon all concerned. The sole outcome of the conference was a meaningless list of innumerable qualities that a deaf-blind person requires to qualify for employment and an equally useless list of countless items that should be included in training. Yet, what was desperately needed (and still is) in service to deaf-blind youth is a creative plan for developing survival strategies in these young people so that they might achieve optimum independence in adult living. In this workshop structure, unfortunately, there was no room for creativity.

So it is in many rehabilitation agencies today. The balance has tipped. In most instances, rehabilitation programs are led by professional administrators whose housekeeping skills are impeccable and whose fiscal acumen merits accolades. But, many of these organizations have become havens for not only administrative types but social bookkeepers as well. Creative professional workers in a number of these organizations have been forced to sublimate their original thinking in favor of safe routines or to seek employment elsewhere. As a consequence, activities at such establishments center around polishing the existing system, closing loopholes, and tightening controls, sometimes to the point of straitjacketing the program. Things are efficient, but not very exciting. Even more important, clients are not receiving the benefit of what was once the most precious resource of rehabilitation—the creative minds of professional practitioners.

The issue is not one of a return to the golden days of yesteryear when idiosyncrasy and invention led to thousands of unprecedented rehabilitation successes. In fact, few agencies could tolerate the "inefficiencies" of the administrators of that day. Yet, at present the load of efficiency laid upon rehabilitation workers by machinelike leaders is generating its own problems. Thus, management in rehabilitation is not an end in itself; it is a means for assisting more disabled persons to attain rehabilitation goals. Can the achievement of such goals occur without creative rehabilitators who are given administrative support in bringing their imaginative ideas to fruition? Then who will take risks to that end, and who will be secure enough to innovate when the case situation calls for it? Thus, the issue now is to find a way to reverse the pendulum so that both the professional administrators and the creative rehabilitation thinkers may coexist and join their separate talents for the ultimate benefit of disabled persons.

Can Voluntary Rehabilitation Agencies Survive As Viable
Participants in the Rehabilitation Service Delivery System?

The federal-state vocational rehabilitation system makes provision
for the active participation of voluntary agencies. Although some state
agencies conduct their own facilities (such as workshops), the overwhelming majority do not, relying instead upon purchasing needed
restoration, evaluation, training, and related services from voluntary
agencies and groups. For the most part, this arrangement has worked
surprisingly well with public and private organizations contributing
their distinctive resources to the combined treatment program. In the
past, voluntary rehabilitation agencies reported that state agency fees
for service constituted a relatively modest proportion of their income.
In those days, public philanthropy, bequests, and other voluntary
support accounted for the bulk of private agency funds. As government
rehabilitation programs grew in size, effectiveness, and importance,
they made greater requests for service from the voluntary agency
sector. Accordingly, voluntary agencies increasingly tailored their
programs to state agency needs and specifications and began to rely to
a growing extent upon state agency fees as a source of income. The
process was hastened by the decline of personal philanthropy in the
United States and the disinclination of many Americans to make
regular and substantial contributions to these groups because of higher
taxes, inflation, and the growing expectation that government, not
charity, would provide essential assistance for less fortunate citizens.
    The consequence of this development was that a close partnership
evolved between state rehabilitation and voluntary agencies. In some
instances, this relationship is so interdependent that the voluntary
agency is almost a quasi-government organization that acts in lieu, and
often, on behalf, of the state rehabilitation agency. In many ways this
has added to the effectiveness of the voluntary sector. For example,
performance standards have been elevated in many communities,
voluntary agencies are better funded than they were, more effective
joint private and government programs are available to disabled
persons almost everywhere, and many medieval practices in the management of some voluntary agencies have been replaced by more appropriate ones. However, the outcomes have not all been felicitous.

Indeed, the blessings have been mixed and, as government continues to expand its role in rehabilitation service, the cracks in the structure are becoming more evident.

Some of the problems emerging from this often harmonious, but sometimes uneasy, private-public agency partnership include: some voluntary organizations have become so dependent upon state agency fees for service that the withdrawal of such fees could bring a voluntary group to the brink of bankruptcy, a fiscal fact of life that often makes the voluntary agency subordinate and, sometimes, obsequious to the public agency; and voluntary agencies long have prided themselves on their independence and their readiness to innovate and experiment in areas in which government cannot, a status that is harder to realize in an interagency climate that sometimes requires the voluntary agency to obtain state agency approval of the personnel they plan to hire. Furthermore, in the programs they plan to launch, and the populations they plan to serve, public agencies may, in the interests of setting higher standards, impose a degree of conformity and conventionality upon voluntary agencies that would have been unthinkable in the not-too-distant past.

The present trend is clearly for public agencies to reshape voluntary agencies, often in their own image. Thus, private agencies are finding it more difficult to accept and work with disabled persons who are not concurrently clients of the public agency. In accepting public agency fees, the voluntary agency often uses state agency-prescribed forms and procedures, accepts the public agency view of the respective roles of the public agency and voluntary agency counselor, and, not infrequently, is required to implement plans developed and prescribed for it by the public agency. Perhaps, this is all to the good, and, perhaps, this trend will lead to eventual nationalization of voluntary agencies. But, if this occurs, the possible losses that could be incurred are worth considering. Among these losses may be a sufficient leeway to experiment and innovate, freedom to work with clients who fall outside eligibility and feasibility boundaries of state agencies, as well as risk-taking and the freedom to develop creative solutions for client problems. These voluntary agency functions are in danger of being deemphasized or even eliminated. Thus, the issue to be decided in the years ahead is: Can a system be devised through which voluntary agencies enter into co-equal partnership with government agencies which insures freedom of private groups to do their own thing without possible retribution?

Concurrently, should the present trend toward government agency dominance be permitted to run its course even if voluntary agencies are swallowed up in the process? By historical accident, some states have virtually no private rehabilitation centers, workshops, or other facilities. Should this become the pattern of tomorrow for the nation?

Should the Term Vocational Remain in Vocational Rehabilitation?

A review of the Vocational Rehabilitation Acts of 1973 and 1974 reveals that the word *vocational* has been dropped from the titles of these acts and from certain key sections of them. This is no accident. Many rehabilitation specialists have long felt that a vocationally oriented rehabilitation program is too restrictive in that it makes it difficult, if not impossible, for the most severely and least vocationally motivated disabled individuals to qualify for, and benefit from, rehabilitation programming. Consequently, great pressure has been exerted on legislators and rehabilitation administrators to take a broader view of rehabilitation subsumed under such titles as independent living, social rehabilitation, self-development, and personal growth. Underscoring this movement has been the feeling that modified current vocational rehabilitation concepts and resources have great potential for disabled persons who either will not or cannot enter into some form of remunerative employment, homemaking, or study leading to employment. Expansion of rehabilitation into areas of personal and social development without reference to employment has seemed to many to be an attractive and logical extension of the rehabilitation movement that could bring substantial benefits to the disabled person, his or her family, and the community and nation as a whole.

Arrayed against this viewpoint is another group of rehabilitation specialists who believe that the current program owes its special status and unprecedented success to its focus upon employment as an end goal. They point to the flounderings of other types of helping programs which have addressed themselves to less tangible service objectives, such as independence, family harmony, social adaptation, and community adjustment. With its clear target of employment and its well-defined services, vocational rehabilitation, they argue, has been able to attain most of its ends. They note that this has been done while simultaneously attracting public and government commendation for running a "tight," fiscally justified and time-tested program that produces measurably significant results. This rehabilitation group believes that the job focus of modern vocational rehabilitation has enabled it to avoid the excesses experienced in such more recently developed programs as the antipoverty effort, the welfare program, and some untargeted revenue-sharing situations. Indeed, it is sometimes felt that if personal and social rehabilitation were to be joined with vocational rehabilitation, the latter would soon be dominated by the former and rehabilitation personnel would readily give priority to nonvocational cases which demand less accountability for rehabilitation accomplishment and which do not require intensive, time-consuming, and foot-wearying placement efforts. In their view, "bad" rehabilitation (that is, rehabilitation that does not result in the attainment of clear-cut specific goals) would soon drive out "good" rehabilitation which produces wage earners and responsible citizens.

As the years go by, social and personal rehabilitation seem to be advancing upon the vocational rehabilitation field. Already, evidences of this change are appearing in legislation, agency procedures, and long-range program plans. The central issue is: Will the unique character and special contributions of the present-day vocational rehabilitation program be lost or, conversely, enhanced in the wake of this development? At the moment, undercurrents of controversy are beginning to be felt and some resistance is being expressed toward the inexorable advance of personal and social rehabilitation. Sooner or later, the advocates of the two viewpoints noted above will interact more fully and the issue will be opened more widely for examination, discussion, and resolution.

Should Present Evidences of Discrimination Against Certain Groups of Disabled Persons Be Retained in the Present Rehabilitation Program?

The picture of rehabilitation discrimination throughout the United States against certain disability groups is very uneven. However, there are states and communities in which older disabled, mentally retarded trainable, severely emotionally disabled, institutionalized, severely and multihandicapped individuals, among others, cannot obtain rehabilitation services even though they are presumably legally and

ethically eligible for them. For example, although rehabilitation legislation, state rehabilitation plans, and stated agency procedures do not
stipulate limitations upon service to individuals fifty-five years of age
and over, literally millions of these individuals are not receiving
needed assistance at this time. Although most homebound people
clearly qualify for assistance, fewer than 5 percent are currently receiving vocational rehabilitation. It would be unproductive to specu-
late about the personal prejudices of rehabilitation leaders and
practitioners. Whether bias springs from the hearts of human beings
or from some unfortunate conjuncture of events and conditions, the
fact is that a disproportionate number of poor, severely limited, and
socially disadvantaged clients or potential clients now fail to obtain
the benefits of rehabilitation.

In some cases, this may be attributed to cultural lag deterrents
described earlier. That is, some rehabilitation agencies have not kept
up to date and, as in the case of the homebound, do not yet realize that
the rehabilitation of such clients is feasible within the current rehabilitation structure. Beyond cultural lag, however, another and even more
dangerous phenomenon is occurring that is sharpening the issue. In
view of the very extensive need of millions of disabled persons for
rehabilitation service and the finite financial resources that are available at any time to operate programs to meet these needs, rehabilitation agencies have been confronted by the unpleasant task of
channeling their resources in some directions and not in others. In the
main, this has been done through setting priorities. Thus, at any one
time, a rehabilitation agency may have explicitly or implicitly committed itself to concentration upon certain groups and not upon others.
The net effect of this has been the establishment of a hierarchy within
the disability groups which renders some of them favored and others
not. Since these priorities change from time to time (often without
apparent reason), the unfavored groups may hope to become the elite
some day, but they are never sure if they will. Changes in priority often
are at variance with the merits of the case presented by a disability
group and may occur because of the activities of a powerful and
distinguished advocate, the infusion of funds designed for a certain
categorical class of persons (such as the poor), or legislative event. On
occasion, a group rises in priority by reason of a trade-off. Thus, in
several communities homebound persons received greater attention
because a handful of their advocates were willing to help the com-

munity in other ways in exchange for assigning a higher priority to this group.

Priorities by disability often make sense to administrators who are hard pressed to meet all the requests for service that are being made on their agencies. Such administrators often use the most rational and democratic methods they can devise to establish their priorities, but try as they may, priorities often culminate in a form of discrimination against resultant low-priority groups. The central issue is: Is the priority form of discrimination in rehabilitation tolerable and practical in the light of current funding conditions and the limits to which public support can be mobilized for rehabilitation or, regardless of current realities, is this system so blatantly prejudicial that it should be eliminated? As rehabilitation consumers acquire a greater voice in rehabilitation matters, they are likely to raise additional questions about disability priorities, and, already, rehabilitation practitioners are indicating a disinclination to accept the premises of a priority system. Undoubtedly, the rising emphasis on human rights that currently pervades American society will cast a stronger spotlight on discrimination in rehabilitation and, perhaps, lead to more equitable ways of husbanding and allocating fiscal resources.

A Closing Word

The issues discussed above are real. Whether we will it or not, they are with us in our everyday rehabilitation experience. In fact, some problems are growing so rapidly in importance that their resolution cannot be delayed much longer. In the past, issues such as these were all too often resolved by default, inaction, or closed-door decisions by a handful of leaders. Although many of the resolutions reached in these ways are commendable, some are not. The only way in which we can be sure that current issues will be resolved in a constructive fashion that enhances and extends the quality and quantity of our service to disabled persons is for us to participate actively and fully in the resolution process. It is not too early for students, practitioners, administrators, and the public to discuss them thoroughly so that all sides can be examined, evaluated, and a worthwhile solution to each problem may be reached.

IMPLICATIONS FOR REHABILITATION PRACTICE

This chapter posed seven issues whose resolution could have important implications for the future of rehabilitation practice.

(1) Does rehabilitation need a theory?
     Pro - Theory generates new understandings of the rehabilitation process and leads to improvements and innovations.
     Con - Theory has little effect on day-to-day practice, and is unrelated to the day-to-day experiences of rehabilitation workers in recent years.

(2) Is the present vocational rehabilitation service delivery system the most favorable one that can be devised?
     Pro - The soundness of the original rehabilitation service delivery concept is supported by the high degree of success achieved in rehabilitating disabled people and in extending and altering procedures.
     Con - There is a need for a major overhaul of the system so that we can better serve the millions of disabled individuals who have severe limitations. Today, the less severely disabled receive a disproportionately high incidence of service under the present system while the severely disabled receive less adequate assistance. Recent setbacks in funding and political support suggest that there are basic weaknesses in the present system.

(3) Can the gap between research and application of research be closed?
     Pro - A variety of research utilization techniques have been devised, but utilization has been deterred by environmental factors, for example, funding, professionals, and rehabilitation leaders are assuming responsibility for applying research findings and with greater support will do a better job of it.
     Con - There are rehabilitation workers who deny that behavioral scientists can produce much of value for the rehabilitation movement. For them, day-to-day experience produces progress, as slow as that may be. Research funds can be better used for

additional service. The real deterrent to research utilization, thus, may be worker attitudes rather than public support.

(4) Shall the rehabilitation movement be led by professional administrators?

Pro - Conducting large agency business and program enterprises requires managerial knowledge and skills such as budgeting, cost accounting, personnel administration, and systems analysis. Such skills are found primarily in administrators trained in the ways of business management.

Con - The advent of orderly, systematic management processes has resulted in the loss of ingenuity, creativity, and intuitive approaches to rehabilitation. Too much of rehabilitation is viewed in business, rather than human terms.

(5) Can voluntary rehabilitation agencies survive in the present delivery system?

Pro - Voluntary agencies are used as providers of services for state agencies. The payment for such services accounts for the bulk of private agency funds and assists in fostering the growth and effectiveness of the voluntary field.

Con - The increase in governmental funding has led to a lessening of private funds and a greater dependence of voluntary rehabilitation agencies on the federal-state system for survival. In becoming quasi-governmental organizations, voluntary agencies have sacrificed such important initiatives as working with disabled individuals not accepted as clients by state agencies and developing experimental and innovative programs that might seem "chancy" by traditional accountability standards. If the trend continues, voluntary agencies may be swallowed up and cease to exist.

(6) Should the term vocational remain in vocational rehabilitation?

Pro - The success of vocational rehabilitation hinges on its employment focus. Moving disabled individuals from a financially dependent status to that of self-supporting, tax-paying citizens has generated the growing public support that has resulted in the present federal-state system.

Con - There are large numbers of disabled people, especially the severely handicapped, who either will not or cannot enter into remunerative employment, homemaking, or study leading to employment. Many rehabilitation workers feel that programs of personal and social development without reference to employment is a logical extension of the present rehabilitation system and should be incorporated by law.

(7)   Are certain groups of disabled persons discriminated against? *Pro* - There are states and communities in which older disabled, mentally retarded trainable, severely emotionally disabled, institutionalized, and severely handicapped individuals cannot obtain rehabilitation services. Fewer than 5 percent homebound people who qualify for assistance are currently receiving vocational rehabilitation. Are they being discriminated against? Why?
Con - The pressure of reduced funds at a time of new and larger rehabilitation populations has caused agencies to channel their resources and make unpleasant priority decisions. Important political elements in our society are calling for greater accountability in governmental spending and this inhibits agency experimentation and working with clients with questionable vocational potential.

These are seven important issues in need of resolution. What is your stand on them? Can we do something about them? Perhaps you would like to communicate your views in the professional literature.

CHAPTER II

A PERSONALIZED RECENT
HISTORY OF VOCATIONAL REHABILITATION
IN AMERICA

SETTING THE SCENE

The author of this chapter, Herbert Rusalem, set out to write a different kind of history of vocational rehabilitation, based in part on his own interpretation of past and present events and social conditions. Typically, other historical accounts present such facts as that Spartan children who were born with physical defects were left on Mount Taygetus to perish from exposure. Or that in 1760 the first public school for deaf children was founded in Paris by Abbé Charles Michel de l'Epée, and so on. Any references to American political figures or parties were studiously avoided as topics considered too hot to handle.

There was good reason for this careful avoidance of political reference in the past. For decades rehabilitation was a popular American movement favored by increasing budgets for facilities, research, training and service, regardless of which party was in power. However, beginning with the late 1960s, a changing governmental leadership and a pernicious inflation wrought a change in political attitude toward the needs of rehabilitation clients and programs. Along with other social and antipoverty programs, rehabilitation projects were perceived as expendable, "luxury" items that could be shelved in a tightening economy. It became more important to fight wars in Vietnam and Cambodia than to rehabilitate millions of American people disabled by physical, emotional, and social conditions. The time had come for the rehabilitation movement to join large numbers of other Americans in protest against the government's current ordering of priorities.

In discussing the recent history of vocational rehabilitation in a frank and candid manner, Rusalem is calling for a new approach by the rehabilitation movement. The era of passive neutralism has come to an end and must be replaced by a forthright partisanship. The needs of disabled individuals are urgent and deserve the attention of the American people. It is up to us—clients, professionals, workers, and administrators—to see to it that these problems are brought before the people and their legislative representatives for resolution.

CHAPTER II

A PERSONALIZED RECENT HISTORY OF
VOCATIONAL REHABILITATION IN AMERICA

HERBERT RUSALEM

The frontier concept has been a dominant theme in American life since the founding of the republic in 1787. At first, the frontier was a geographical one, with the vast undeveloped lands to the West offering unbounded opportunities and serving as a safety valve for the feeling of many disadvantaged and unsuccessful people. As long as this alternate way of life existed, the prevailing mood of the country continued to be hopeful, energetic, and expansionist. When the influence of the geographical frontier psychology began to wane in the late nineteenth century, this development coincided with the onrush of the new technological revolution. With open lands no longer available, the country's new frontier became America's seemingly limitless industrial opportunities.

Through the new medium of employment opportunities in industrial and business enterprises, disadvantaged Americans found a new and equally promising frontier working for, managing, and sometimes owning profit-making enterprises of all sizes and types. In many instances, these emerging enterprises rewarded ingenuity, creativity, drive, and sustained effort with unprecedented economic benefits. Thus, during the late nineteenth century and well into the middle of the twentieth, the dream of going West was effectively replaced by the dream of climbing up capitalism's success ladder. In effect, advancement in business became the new frontier, the avenue through which disadvantaged citizens and immigrants could hope to attain a quality of life that was well beyond the dreams of their parents. Just as the open-land frontier stoked the motivations of Americans in its time, the industrial frontier that succeeded it fanned the flames of ambition among the poor and disabled in its own way. In keeping with the then popular Horatio Alger-like overly optimistic view of this newer frontier, productivity, initiative, loyalty to one's employer, and good work habits were the tools with which poor persons could fashion a middle class lifestyle.

As the twentieth century progressed, it became increasingly clear that the industrial frontier, now dominated by vast multinational companies, was closing, as the opportunities for individual ʾupward mobility in the business establishment became less available to the working man, let alone the poor and the disadvantaged. More and more, union membership and governmental intervention replaced company conformity as the preferred pathway to economic security. Concurrently, higher educational requirements became routine for upper echelon positions, and executive suites were being occupied increasingly by those who had acquired social graces, accepted modes of communication, and the polish of middle class mores. Indeed, business advancements came to depend upon lengthy apprenticeships in how to become an effective "team" member in the "gray flannel" establishment, rather than on the rugged buccaneer qualities of the self-made leaders of an earlier generation.

While industrial leadership opportunities were being reserved for the educated and the socially sophisticated, a new humanistic frontier was emerging. Stirred by the privations suffered by the poor during the great depressions of the twentieth century, national policy began to reveal a greater compassion for the "common man," as America found extreme poverty in the midst of affluence less acceptable to the national conscience. It became apparent that individual charity and foundation philanthropy were not equal to the task of coping with the massive financial, educational, health, and social needs of the poor and the disabled. Only the power and resources of central government were sufficient to reverse the unprecedented distress that accompanied a wildly cyclical economy.

In 1902, with the passage of the first Workmen's Compensation legislation (Obermann, 1965) for injured workmen in Maryland and subsequent related enactments throughout the United States, the American humanistic revolution was launched and public policy moved toward direct federal intervention to correct the inequities suffered by disabled and deprived citizens. Earlier, government involvement in social issues (starting early in the nineteenth century with the development of tariffs) had consisted primarily of delivering "welfare" benefits to affluent capitalists while contemporaneously deifying free enterprise and open competition. Thus, for more than 100 years, welfare and rehabilitation programs served the well-to-do almost exclusively. In fact, it was considered heretical, radical, and almost atheistic to suggest that the proper recipients of government welfare programs really should be the poor rather than the affluent. Underlying this stand was the belief that the poor were poor because of defects in their character and that government benefits would only extend these defects and encourage sloth and dependency.

During and after World War I, the nation first became aware of the social and vocational potentials of severely disabled veterans through meeting and hearing about wounded servicemen who had been helped by rehabilitation programs conducted under the auspices of the Armed Forces and the Veterans Administration (U.S. Congress, 1918). Consequently, despite the then prevailing attitudes of rugged individualism, states such as Wisconsin, Nevada, and California took initial steps in 1918 and 1919 to test a more humanistic view of government functions by offering rehabilitation-related services, first to the industrially injured and, then, to other disabled persons. After much debate and several temporary setbacks, the humanist frontier really opened wide on the federal level when Public Law 236 (The Vocational Rehabilitation Act of 1920) was passed by the Sixty-sixth Congress and signed into law by President Woodrow Wilson on June 2, 1920. This Act established the Federal-State Vocational Rehabilitation Program which is today, as it was then, the keystone of American rehabilitation—an early, and still viable, expression of an American humanistic philosophy (U.S. Congress, 1920).

The creation of a Federal-State-Voluntary Agency Program partnership for the purpose of rehabilitating disabled people was so revolutionary that the system took root slowly. However, the soundness of the original concept was confirmed year after year and even though the program has had a number of amendments, expansions, and additions, its basic original philosophy structure articulated by Congress in the 1920 legislation remains as relevant to today's problems as to those of 50 years ago. Attacks upon this program in the 1960s and 1970s by mindless management bureaucrats employed by the Nixon Administration did not obscure the fact that this pioneering humanistic program has for more than 50 years demonstrated how really effective government can be in serving disadvantaged citizens. Indeed, the attackers have departed from the seats of power, but the program perseveres. At a hearing conducted by a Congressional Subcommittee, Nixon Administration critics of the Federal-State Vocational Rehabilitation Program were challenged by legislative leaders to provide facts, supporting an HEW memo that advocated discontinuance of the Program. Their large response yielded no philosophical or clinical basis for such a proposal. On the other hand, the continuing bright success of the clearly defined objectives of the Federal-State Vocational Rehabilitation Program with its built-in evaluative criteria related to the employment, earnings, and tax contributions of rehabilitated workers continue to confirm its economic as well as humanistic offectiveness.

In addition to providing the foundation for what has become an extensive multilevel rehabilitation network in the United States, Public Law 236, more generally, opened the way for the emergence of new American attitudes toward human problems. For example, following the implementation of the Vocational Rehabilitation Act of 1920, local, state, and national interest began to coalesce around the idea that a government can and should function as a supportive intervenor in the lives of citizens who endure misfortunes. Despite this newer thinking, the Harding, Coolidge and Hoover Administrations continued to place the interests of business before those of people so that the idea of rehabilitating disadvantaged individuals remained more of a promise than a fulfillment. When the great depression of the 1930s sent shock waves reverberating throughout every corner of the United States, the time was ripe for a major shift in governmental priorities. Gradually, the Federal-State Vocational Rehabilitation Program grew and, concomitantly, a number of other human service programs were initiated in such areas as welfare, social security, unemployment insurance, and housing. These new programs could not be thwarted indefinitely by advocates of governmental welfare benefits for business and contemporaneous detachment from people.

In conjunction with the extension of this new human frontier, dating from approximately 1920 through the Lyndon Johnson Administration in the mid-1960s, the Federal-State Vocational Rehabilitation Program was periodically strengthened by amendments (as in 1943 and 1954) and by changes in administrative procedures (Ober-

mann, 1965). Since the movement toward more comprehensive rehabilitation programming was progressively helpful to disadvantaged
individuals and the nation as a whole, it received extensive support
from most segments of American society. It was not unusual for rehabilitation proposals to receive almost universal legislative approval
from conservatives, moderates, and liberals. Indeed, it sometimes
seemed that politicians were vying with each other in their professions
of faith in rehabilitation. In time, new definitions of disability, eligibility, and feasibility and more liberal interpretations of national and
state legislation added impetus to the movement and reinforced the
concept that vocational rehabilitation is very much in the national
interest. Consequently, there was an almost continual enrichment of
rehabilitation during the 1950s and 1960s and a steady expansion in
services for new and existing client populations (including the mentally retarded and the emotionally disabled). Additional evidences of
growth appeared in such areas as the increasing level of public fiscal
support, the introduction of research and professional training components, and the provision of physical and emotional restoration along
with supportive workshop experiences as part of a total rehabilitation
process. Furthermore, social disabilities such as alcoholism, drug ad-
diction, and legal offenders were reached by rehabilitation programs
with increasing regularity and effectiveness.

At mid-twentieth century, when the human frontier was at its ze-
nith, rehabilitation crackled with excitement. Notable leaders, such as
Mary Switzer and Jim Garrett, emerged, a new flexibility and a new
responsiveness to individuality were manifested, significant advances
were made in programming, impressive demonstrations were
launched, and, most important of all, more disabled persons than ever
before were receiving a broader spectrum of appropriate rehabilitation
interventions. Simultaneously, the private agency sector, led by administrators such as Milt Cohen of the Federation of the Handicapped,
was expanding markedly as well, often stimulated by grants, encouragement, and ideational support from federal and state rehabilitation
agencies. Hospitals, rehabilitation centers, community agencies, sheltered workshops, and other facilities were founded and expanded in
growing numbers, and in a vast humanistic outburst of energy, they
flourished as never before. These voluntary organizations uniformly
established partnerships with state rehabilitation agencies so that the
contributions of both private and public sectors could be maximized

and coordinated for the benefit of disabled persons. Not infrequently, voluntary agencies formed the outer edge of new rehabilitation practices, entering into unexplored programmatic areas when governmental structures made it difficult to do so. In general, the mid-twentieth century was the golden age of American rehabilitation because this field was in the forefront of community consciousness, and unprecedented leadership galvanized community support for wider rehabilitation boundaries.

During the 1950s, a national concern developed concerning America's capacity to cope with the growing strength of the Soviet Union. Diplomatic setbacks, fear of communist infiltration at home and abroad, Soviet successes in atomic energy, military adventures, and space activities, coupled with a weakening of national pride and purpose, generated a shift of emphasis away from people in the direction of science. Thus, a new scientific frontier, which spread far beyond the borders of traditional science, emerged. For example, management sciences were enthroned in many seats of power, displacing the humanists and their "tarnished" programs for perfecting the human condition. Computers became oracles, and those who tended them became an administrative elite. The objective of this new scientific frontier was the rational control of organizational behaviors and systems, rather than the facilitation of individual welfare and development among the disabled and the disadvantaged. For a time vocational rehabilitation coexisted amicably with the managers of the technological-managerial frontier because rehabilitation leaders retained their essential commitment to human rehabilitation and exercised sufficient influence in the power structure to withstand the assaults of the new managerial breed in government. However, in the mid-1960s, evidences of retreat became apparent as rehabilitation budgets were targeted for cuts and, for the first time, economists, business people, and middle management bureaucrats felt secure enough as products of their times to question some of the most basic assumptions of rehabilitation. The culmination of this phenomenon occurred in 1973 when the eminent economist Eli Ginzberg of Columbia University declared in a lead article in the Teachers College Record that the expenditure of public funds to vocationally rehabilitate severely disabled persons was a policy of dubious validity in an era of marked unemployment among the nondisabled. Indeed, argued Ginzberg, the nation might be better served by offering such persons a form of social rehabilitation that does not prepare them to compete in an already glutted labor market.

At about this time, the government managerial technocrats were talking about assessing social and humanistic programs in terms of economic outcomes. In this view, it was felt that government and voluntary groups should measure the costs of various human services in the light of the "hard" (measurable) benefits obtained from them. Through comparing fiscal input and output data, it would be possible, they claimed, to make a judgment concerning the values to the nation of various programs of social betterment. In a period of rising taxes and widespread inflation, when national government expenditures for social services are second only to defense commitments, the idea of more rigorous fiscal justification of social programs took root particularly in conservative, economic, and political circles. It was implied that the nation had already gone too far in its efforts to assist the disabled and the disadvantaged to attain more fruitful lives. Undoubtedly, the advocates of this ideology helped substantially to elect Richard M. Nixon to the Presidency. "Fiscal integrity," a commitment to welfare programs for big business and an insensitivity to the problems of the poor and the disabled, generally characterized the Nixon Administration from its inception. Soon after the 1968 election, Nixon surrounded himself with people who viewed power, not human betterment, as the major concern of government and its leaders.

The succession of dehumanizing policies and events that preceded and followed Watergate, which ultimately culminated in Nixon's resignation, had an important impact on rehabilitation, transforming the golden age to the darker days of the 1970s. More or less compliant, but thoroughly loyal officials were shuffled in and out of government rehabilitation offices with monotonous regularity and, with few exceptions, these office-holders had little commitment to rehabilitation. Many of these faithful retainers were Nixon-supporting businessmen, bookkeepers, budget-watchers, political hacks, and nondescript conservatives who somehow had gained the attention of the White House staff. Looking back at this period, one concludes that if the ultimate goal of the Administration was to dismantle the Federal-State Vocational Rehabilitation Program, better qualified dismemberment personnel could not have been selected. With the encouragement of the White House, but contrary to the manifest wishes of the Congress, these retreaded leaders allied themselves with the gospel of cost-effectiveness, economy, arbitrary priorities, and constriction of humaneness in dealing with disabled persons. One of the corollary problems of this period was that some politically oriented state and voluntary rehabilitation agency leaders not only applied systems notions to rehabilitation service, but, in some cases, became erstwhile apostles of and apologists for this approach. Admittedly, it was safe to do so in the political climate of that time. But, the managers and their rehabilitation collaborators violated what rehabilitation is all about—that is, a humane and individualized service that considers every disabled person to be surpassing in his value as a human being and deserving of all government assistance that can be given, regardless of tightening budgets and exclusionary priorities.

The consequences of the constrictive managerial approach, while in harmony with an administration that ran roughshod over individual rights, were disastrous for many disabled people. Unreasonable priority systems were set up that placed clients in layers. Those who were considered more worthy according to some indefinable criterion (perhaps their potential or promise to become substantial earners and taxpayers with relatively little trouble or cost) were placed in the upper layers and were given early and fuller access to rehabilitation services. On the other hand, those with multiple and challenging problems tended to fall to the bottom of the priority heap and were generally excluded from the full benefits of rehabilitation. This elitist system should be contrasted with the traditional "open-door" policy of the rehabilitation movement which granted almost every eligible disabled person an opportunity to enter, and benefit from, the program.

Other evidences of contraction and restriction that began to appear during the Nixon years included:

- Instead of being expanded to meet the growing need for skilled rehabilitation personnel, professional training programs were allotted declining support and, in some cases, were actually phased out.
- Rehabilitation research, which had yielded such a rich load of new and improved rehabilitation practices in the 1950s and 1960s, was cut back ruthlessly and, for the most part, still languishes in some second-order bureaucratic pattern.
- States that had been service-oriented also began to manage their

rehabilitation establishments on the basis of economy rather than usefulness to disabled people. Not infrequently, a denying attitude replaced the earlier exhilarating desire to help, which had made rehabilitation great. It finally got to the point in some states that severely disabled applicants had to justify their claim on state rehabilitation services rather than, as had been the case earlier, being sought out for service by the Program. At times during this period, state agencies prided themselves on how much unspent funds were being turned back to the national and state treasuries rather than on how effective they were in solving the disability problems of their communities.

- In order to obtain the attenuated grants that still were available, voluntary agencies at the state and local level were compelled to go through the process of attempting to justify their proposals in terms of presumed savings that would accrue to federal and state government, rather than benefit the disabled.

- In 1970, for the first time in history, not one, but two acts passed by the Congress for the improvement of the Federal-State Vocational Rehabilitation Program were vetoed by an American President. It is to the credit of the Congress that, in the face of the callous insensitivity of an essentially antihuman administration, it held firm to its resolve. A bill was passed and signed by the President that accomplished some, if not all, of their objectives for the disabled.

- Rehabilitation-related activities were assigned in some cases to nonrehabilitation agencies. For example, antipoverty programs that were administered by manpower or Office of Economic Opportunity groups, which had had little experience and even less distinction in the rehabilitation arena. Similarly, rehabilitation-oriented programs for the aging, narcotics addicts, alcoholics, the emotionally ill, and the mentally retarded were established independent of existing rehabilitation agency structures on the federal, and in some cases, the state level. In time, voluntary rehabilitation agencies found that a considerable proportion of the fiscal support received for their rehabilitation programs was emanating not so so much from the Federal-State Rehabilitation Program as from mental health, mental retardation, social security, welfare, and manpower funding agencies. In a real sense, it became evident that rehabilitation responsibilities that had once centralized on the federal level, at least, were being distributed to a broad range of federal nonrehabilitation groups and that the status of national government-sponsored rehabilitation in America was being systematically chipped away.

• Proposals were made by the Nixon Administration representatives to incorporate federal support of state and local vocational rehabilitation programs into revenue-sharing, thereby exposing the rehabilitation program to compete locally for funds with a host of other programs and making the program subject to political pressures and local whim. This would almost certainly have reduced the effectiveness of American rehabilitation and left the program subject to local priorities, including waste disposal, law enforcement, fire protection, poverty, and housing.

The scope of this critical event by the Nixon Administration to dehumanize and dismember this highly durable and functional federal-state rehabilitation system is suggested by the proceedings of the aforementioned hearing by the House Subcommittee chaired by Representative Brademas. At one session, an internal HEW Departmental memo was made public, which recommended that the painstakingly developed professionally staffed Federal-State Vocational Rehabilitation Program should be replaced by a system of grants to individual disabled persons with which they could purchase local rehabilitation services. Members of the Subcommittee sharply challenged statements made by Administration representatives that the Federal-State Voluntary Agency Program was failing to fulfill its objectives and was in need of total overhaul. On the contrary, the Subcommittee noted the essential well-being of the current program despite the fact that Administration maneuvers had been whittling away at it for a number of years. This encounter, coupled with the Nixon Administration's cavalier handling of many other HEW rehabilitation programs, unfortunately failed to generate the widespread professional indignation that it deserved. Thus, while the Administration made move after move to undermine the Program, many rehabilitation leaders stood by passively at a time when concerted action to cope with peril was indicated. All too many rehabilitation leaders tacitly acquiesced or took to the sidelines while a few of them participated in concerted counterattacks. One bright spot was that this prevailing passivity was recognized by disabled persons in all parts of the country, some of whom helped to organize and lead grass roots client-directed movements that forcefully spoke out for the disabled at a time when their interests were in grave peril.

On balance, the Nixon Presidency was not one of the brightest periods in the history of American rehabilitation. With few exceptions, rehabilitation agency administrators accepted the "new order," professional organizations were generally cautious, and the universities interested in rehabilitation mounted no campaigns to save the Program. When Gerald Ford assumed the Presidency, the recession and its consequent deficit budgets and reductions in expenditures for human services left little room for optimism. The crucial element will be whether the rehabilitation movement has learned from this recent experience. If rehabilitation administrators, professional workers, and clients continue to yield to political expediency and political maneuvering, if they do not rise to defend and extend the basic tenet that rehabilitation serves *all* eligible disabled persons in an effective, understanding, and dignified fashion, and if they fail to aggressively propose creative new approaches that will strengthen and invigorate the existing program, changes in the Presidency will make little difference. In periods of low economic activity, the dismantling process may be stepped up unless the passivity, stagnation, and dry rot in the movement can be cut away. The story of rehabilitation is built upon the deeds of courageous pioneers who did not fear to confront deleterious entrenched dogmas and power structures. Few such leaders are now among us. Until more of them appear with bright new ideas to reawaken this field to its traditions, the prognosis for rehabilitation remains clouded.

Current Status

The rehabilitation movement in the United States is a highly durable social phenomenon that has withstood recent attacks without undergoing major attenuation. Today, more disabled persons than ever are being served, attention is increasingly being directed toward clients with multiple and difficult problems; although rehabilitation workers sometimes have morale problems, they are the best trained rehabilitation personnel in our history; rehabilitation facilities, such as rehabilitation centers, sheltered workshops, general and special hospitals,

and work activity and day care centers, are more sophisticated than in
the past; and public and legislative commitment to support rehabilitation programs is still ours to grasp. The quality, diversity, effectiveness, and dedication of rehabilitation workers is still impressive,
although progressive change is needed in all of these areas. In brief,
rehabilitation is alive and well. In order to stay that way, it will have to
keep moving forward or succumb to hardening of its organizational
and service arteries. Possible directions for the present and future
growth can be focused out of an understanding of the current status of
the rehabilitation movement. Listed below are some present distinguishing attributes of this field:

1. Crystallization. After a period of rapid expansion and innovation,
the rehabilitation field is settling into a period of modest and gradual
growth. The glamor and tensions of rapid proliferation and startling
expansion are no longer with us. Relatively quiet stability has become
a dominant feeling tone in a field that now is more certain of what it is
than of what it should become. Thus, the prevailing mood in rehabilitation is one of consolidation rather than experimentation and, in
some quarters, one may even detect the coalescing of dogma. For
example, the values of orthodox client evaluation, counseling, and
training are accepted virtually without question as essential ingredients in the rehabilitation process. Yet, there is good reason to reex-
amine and, perhaps, revise the processes drastically. Dramatic change
may yet come, but the current mood in the field suggests that is not
imminent. With the exception of a few agencies like the Federation of
the Handicapped, rehabilitation programs are settling back into
well-worn ways.

2. A Turning-Out. In the past, rehabilitation in the United States
was almost a self-contained system. Most aspects of the rehabilitation
process found their expression through the cooperative federal-state
voluntary agency system and, indeed, rehabilitation personnel constituted an in-group family of closely interlocked workers. As funds for
direct rehabilitation functions and agency facilities were reduced at
the hands of the Nixon Administration, some agency administrators
found it necessary to relate more closely to manpower, mental health,
anti-poverty, mental retardation, and educational institutions and
programs, finding therein opportunities for expanded services that

were being blocked in the rehabilitation establishment. Thus, for good or bad, rehabilitation functions today are more widely distributed than ever before. In place of a centralized rehabilitation effort, funds are being derived from a variety of sources; rehabilitation programs are emerging from other federal and state agencies; rehabilitation workers are finding jobs in settings that in the past were not part of the rehabilitation system; and problems of duplication, overlap, and coordination are occurring with greater frequency.

3. Change in Emphasis. Earlier in its history, American vocational rehabilitation was conducted primarily for the physically disabled, middle-class client, and used the office-centered therapeutic counseling model to achieve employment goals. In recent years, the changing rehabilitation caseload has become more representative of the mentally retarded and emotionally disabled, with increasing proportions of economically and socially disadvantaged clients who require outreach community-based services, environmental and behavioral counseling, and counselor involvement advocacy and interdisciplinary team work. Continuing into the present, these trends are occurring in the context of large caseloads per counselor, the traditionalism of some rehabilitation administrators and counselors, and the conservatism of some states and localities. Despite these factors, the changes noted above persist in their almost irresistible advance. Rehabilitation is changing whether rehabilitation workers want it or not. The question is whether it will be imposed upon us or whether we will have the courage and the foresight to participate in shaping it.

4. The Utilization Crisis. As part of the aging process, rehabilitation structures have become harder to penetrate with the result that new and experimental ideas are running into greater resistance. Indeed, the exciting findings of some research and demonstration projects conducted 10 to 20 years ago have not yet been utilized substantially by rehabilitation agencies in their day-to-day operations. Examples include conclusive evidence that homebound persons can be served successfully and economically in the present system, that older handicapped workers have enormous rehabilitation potential, that vocational rehabilitation is the treatment of choice for many emotionally disabled persons, and that mentally retarded individuals can qualify for more challenging higher-level jobs than are currently open to them.

The rehabilitation field has not yet found the means through which administrators and practitioners can be more effectively informed about these findings. More important, we do not yet have the tools to overcome resistance to change. That fact causes many workers in the field to cling to familiar but outmoded practices. Closely aligned to this problem is the observation that emerging promising procedures show little sign of being incorporated into everyday rehabilitation practice. For example, an analysis by Rusalem and Rusalem indicates that much of rehabilitation is a teaching-learning situation. Yet, only a handful of agencies have incorporated the principles of learning capacities diagnosis and treatment into their regular programs. This lag continues despite the fact that organizations like the Federation of the Handicapped have conclusively demonstrated the relevance of this approach for all clients.

5. *Personnel Imperfections.* Despite its overall usefulness, the rehabilitation agency network is beginning to reveal correctible imperfections that relate to those who work in the service. Included in this category are occasional counselor callousness and stereotyping, ritualistic occupational choices imposed on clients, disinclination to make the client a comanager of the program, emphasis upon numbers of cases rather than quality of service, avoidance of placement activities, undue delays in providing service, limiting rehabilitation goals to early employment rather than career development, avoidance of severely handicapped clients, and lack of counselor imaginativeness and inventiveness. All these conditions require early remediation. The available procedures for dealing with these problems have been only partially effective.

6. *New Client Populations.* With all its limitations, the federal, state, and voluntary agency rehabilitation system remains the most effective tool ever devised to overcome the debilitating effects of physical, intellectual, emotional, and social disabilities. Until relatively recently, the benefits of this system were available primarily to members of the standard disability groups. However, over the years the definition of disability has expanded significantly, so that many who were excluded from the program ten years ago are accepted for service today without reservation. In the years ahead, other groups are likely to be brought into the system in greater numbers, including "nondisabled" socially,

and economically disadvantaged persons, disabled elementary school children, nonhandicapped retirees, school dropouts, and displaced workers. In speculating about the future, one can visualize the possibility of a rehabilitation system that serves everyone. Indeed, in a legalistic sense one finds it hard to justify the delivery of applicable rehabilitation services to just one defined segment of the American population.

A Look Ahead. Until the mid-1960s rehabilitation had compiled a distinguished growth history as one of the American's unique contributions to humanity. The Nixon period may be regarded as a setback that, hopefully, will be only temporary. Certainly, there will be challenges enough in the 1970s and 1980s to bring out the best in the movement. The key to the future lies in leadership. If federal, state, and voluntary agencies select creative leaders to direct rehabilitation in this country—people in the image of the pioneers who made rehabilitation great—the future of rehabilitation in America will be bright indeed. On the other hand, if leadership is put in the hands of political hacks, unimaginative managers, and play-it-safe bureaucrats, American rehabilitation will be put in jeopardy. The history of rehabilitation is the history of its leadership. Thus, rehabilitation workers and their disabled constituents have much at stake in the choice of leadership in this field and should play a part in establishing leadership standards and in participating in the selection of leaders who meet these standards.

BIBLIOGRAPHY

Obermann, E. E. *A History of Vocational Rehabilitation.* Minneapolis: T. S. Denison, 1965.

U.S. Congress, Public Law 178. 65th Congress. Washington, D.C.: 1918.

U.S. Congress. Public Law 236. 66th Congress. Washington D.C.: 1920.

IMPLICATIONS FOR REHABILITATION PRACTICE

American history might be viewed as consisting of a series of frontiers that created opportunities for people. The first frontier was a geographical one which drew to it the "rugged individuals of our society to "conquer" the West. The second was an industrial frontier that saw the rise of American business and industry, and vast opportunities for getting ahead through individual enterprise. The third frontier, a recent one, followed the closing of the industrial domain and is labeled by the author a humanitarian frontier. The humanitarian frontier was a response to individual privation through expanding the role of government in creating a national network of health, educational, and welfare services and programs to assist people in a great variety of ways. This new frontier offered a pathway for millions of people to both serve and be served in the fulfillment of human needs.

The field of vocational rehabilitation came into existance as part of the humanitarian frontier, and in response to the need of tens of thousands of World War I disabled veterans for vocational retraining and job placement. The program for wounded veterans then became a model for an expanded federal-state apparatus created to serve all physically disabled citizens. In time, amendments to the basic law enabled mentally retarded, emotionally disabled and socially disadvantaged individuals to also become eligible for rehabilitation services.

The late 1950s saw the emergence of a fourth frontier, a scientific one that ushered in the space and computer age. With this frontier came not only technological advancement, but also a new class of technocrat-managers. They were individuals, trained in engineering and computer operation, who approached all problems, human as well as nonhuman, with slide rule in hand and formulas in mind. They eventually became the new breed of governmental experts who were moved into all areas of agency management. Their respect for budgets and cost accounting superseded any concern for people and their problems, with the result that the shape of the rehabilitation enterprise began to change significantly. Research and other innovative approaches whose payoff was not readily apparent were cast aside for more pragmatic solutions and for the accumulation of favorable statistics.

In documenting the process that has changed the face and nature of the rehabilitation movement and slowed its growth over the past decade, Rusalem makes a major contribution to our understanding of how to cope with this problem. It is that all rehabilitation professionals have to become more aggressive in "defending the basic concept of serving *all* disabled persons with understanding and dignity." If this means playing politics, naming names, and staging protests at given times, then we must be prepared to do so. As Toynbee reminded society many years ago, those who fail to learn from history are doomed to repeat it.

CHAPTER III

VOCATIONAL DEVELOPMENT PROBLEMS OF THE HANDICAPPED

SETTING THE SCENE

Rehabilitation workers encounter their clients at some point well along the stream of personal development. In many respects, individuals enter rehabilitation as full-blown products of a lifetime of experiences which have shaped their physical, intellectual, emotional, social, and, not the least important from our point of view, vocational attributes. Since a career choice that is compatible with reality and gratifying to disabled persons is essential to the helping process in rehabilitation, workers in this field necessarily are concerned with the processes through which career preferences are expressed and decisions are made. Since all clients bring with them a history of such decisions and choices, their present status can only be fully understood by knowing the developmental sequence which they followed in arriving at this point in their vocational development.

In the past, it was believed by many that the career choice process was chaotic, unplanned, and subject to decisive change factors. As long as this view prevailed, rehabilitation workers built few therapeutic interventions around vocational development. Now, however, it is increasingly clear to most rehabilitation personnel that there is order, sequence, and coherence to career development, and that, in some respects, this development can be influenced by informed and skillful counselors. This chapter will introduce the reader to the fundamentals of the career development process, the special implications of disability and disadvantage for it, and the means that can be used to shape it in a professional relationship. An understanding of these components is central to the evolution of a suitable vocational rehabilitation plan for a client, and, thus, Osipow's observations can be considered a prerequisite for all vocational rehabilitation counseling at all age levels.

CHAPTER III

VOCATIONAL DEVELOPMENT PROBLEMS OF THE HANDICAPPED

Samuel H. Osipow

The study of career development, that is, the manner in which vocational choices develop, are implemented, change, and the satisfactions and frustrations they engender, has been approached with increasing intensity and sophistication during the three decades following the end of World War II. At the end of the war, the principal impetus to study in this area stemmed from a desire to swiftly and justly reintegrate returning war veterans into civilian society and its economy. More recently, the field of career development has become an important aspect of the civil rights movement and the effort of various minority groups to move toward the "good life." Though some minority groups, notably blacks and women, have profited somewhat from career development efforts, other groups, in particular the physically handicapped and disabled, have largely been bypassed by career development researchers, theoreticians, and program developers. Although some attention has been paid to the handicapped by career development workers, the efforts have mostly been offhand and delivered by those few specialists directly concerned with rehabilitating the handicapped.

A principal focus of this chapter is to explore the reasons for this failure to actively apply career development concepts to the disabled, and to attempt to suggest some ways to reverse the current tendency to shortchange the physically handicapped in our thinking about careers and career development. To accomplish these objectives, this chapter will briefly review the major concepts and constructs central to career development theory, explicate the assumptions underlying career de-

51

velopment theory, describe some assumptions that are often made, both implicitly as well as explicitly, about the handicapped, show the points of congruence and incongruence between the two sets of assumptions, and consider the possibility that it is the disparity between the two sets of assumptions (i.e., career development theory and behavior of the disabled) that results in the tendency of vocational psychologists to ignore the disabled. Finally, some suggestions will be made about what should be done to improve the quality of vocational counseling of the disabled and to generate more substantive theoretical work in the field of the vocational rehabilitation of the disabled in terms of systemic variables, such as the educational system, programs, such as counseling efforts, the training of professionals, both in conceptual and practical skills and research possibilities.

Career Development Theory

Until the decade of the 1940s, most of the interest in vocational development was atheoretical, based upon the Parsonian notion of fitting people to work that matches personal characteristics. Not until the post-World War II period were deliberate and concentrated efforts to build concepts about the motivations, process, and outcomes of vocational decisions seriously attempted. During that postwar period, several well-known theorists created systems to describe the process of vocational choice, its implementation, and, to some extent, its progress through the life-span. (These have been extensively described and reviewed in Osipow, 1973.) The theories of Super (1953; 1963), Ginzberg, et al. (1951), Roe (1957), and Holland (1959; 1966; 1973) have emphasized two major ideas: the systematic development of vocational life, and personality implementation through career. For Ginzberg, et al. (1951), systematic development is represented in a series of stages through adolescence into early adulthood that display increasing involvement in decision-making for the world of work; a similar, though more detailed, mechanism describing development was used by Super, except that Super's stages extend throughout the life-span (1953; 1963). For Roe (1957), the developmental period most significantly related to career occurs during the early childhood years when experiences with significant others (especially parents) determine the individual's basic interpersonal orientation and style of need-satisfying efforts in general and in work in particular.

Personality development through career is introduced by Super in terms of self-concept implementation, that is, the notion that all individuals try to display and satisfy their self-view in the work they choose to do and the manner in which they approach it. For Holland, personality implementation through work is simply the attempt of individuals to enter a work environment that is congruent with their personal orientation to the world; individuals, whose personalities are characterized by some idiosyncratic combination of six personality types dominated by one or two of the types, try to find work environments whose settings are populated by people and events like their own dominant traits. For Roe, personality implementation in career is accomplished by the individual's choice of a person- or nonperson-oriented vocation, the choice itself reflecting the individual's personality style.

A great deal of research has been conducted in the context of these four theoretical approaches to career development. Considerable support, at least in broad outline, has been summoned for Super's and Holland's theories, and the stages of Ginzberg's approach seem generally valid. Only Roe's theory has had little support and, even for her work, some recent data (see Osipow, 1973, p. 30) and revisions in the theory (Roe and Klos, 1969) suggest that some validity may exist for her formulation.

Theory as an Ideal. Despite the overall base of empirical support for the theories, as noted elsewhere (Osipow, 1969), the theories represent an "ideal" representation of career development. The theories describe a white, male, middle class professional or managerial world, and have somewhat less to do with the world of the poor, or black, or female, or Spanish-speaking, or disabled. Examined closely, the career development of such people is far less systematic than the theories would suggest, and the nonwhite, nonmale individuals have less opportunity to implement their personality in their work choice than do affluent men. For some nonmajority people, work represents such negative activity because of its context (it is dirty, demeaning, and often both) that to suggest that work represents one's personality may be insulting. Such is not infrequently the situation for blacks (Osipow, 1975a) or females (Osipow, 1975b) who cannot afford to acquire their self-esteem from their work because the work they generally do is so demeaning. As has been shown (Osipow, 1975a), the concepts of developmental stages, self-concept implementation, occupational environments, and personality types do not apply directly to females and poor black males adequately and must be modified or excluded from conceptual schemes designed to explain career development for those groups.

Career Development Assumptions. Some assumptions, however, about career development do appear possible to assert at this time (see Senesh and Osipow, 1973, for amplification):

(1)   Career development is systematic.
(2)   Career development has a psychological basis.
(3)   Career development has a cultural basis.
(4)   The "total" person is involved in career development.
(5)   People possess multipotentiality for careers.
(6)   Career development is sequential and characterized by change.
(7)   Career development is stressful.

In other words, in order to understand the process of career development, it is necessary to postulate some system to encompass vocational life, as well as to have a framework to use in understanding behavior in general. In addition, it is necessary to understand the context (social and economic) in which individuals find themselves. It also appears that it is a mistake to view career life as detached from "personal" life, to search for "one perfect job" that draws upon the individual's characteristics highly efficiently, to strive for an end career result instead of a process is unrealistic, and to fail to recognize the inherent anxieties involved in an individual's prevocational and vocational life is a serious error.

Assumptions About the Disabled. It is common to possess stereotypes about people who have superficial similarities to one another and who differ from the so-called normal or modal population in some significant way. Usually, the stereotypes are negative and represent the modal society's concern with the differences the minority may display. Thus, females are stereotyped as soft, passive, submissive, emotional, and intuitive; blacks as lazy, shiftless, or undependable; Jews as greedy; Scots as miserly; Italians as dishonest; Poles as stupid; Irish as volatile drunks, and so on.

The stereotypes are overgeneralizations about the behaviors and attributes of some members of the minority group, and fail to recognize that the undesirable, stereotyped behaviors are evident in all members of the human race, that their presence is not constant in individuals, but rather situational, and that many members of the majority populations exhibit the minority stereotyped behaviors and vice versa.

Stereotypes of the disabled follow a similar pattern to other stereotypes. People are somewhat frightened of the disabled because the disabled are different from them and remind people of what they might be like. The reminder also induces some varying degrees of guilt feelings in normal individuals for *not* being disabled while others are. Furthermore, overgeneralizations about the disabled are typical because few people bother to really get acquainted with disabled individuals.

Among the stereotypes about the disabled pointed out by Wright (1969) are the myths of the disabled being generally maladjusted and frustrated. There is also the notion that the disability represents a personal tragedy in the life of the disabled individual in retribution for some "sinful" behavior.

It is common to assume that the disabled are all the same as one another with respect to a number of important variables. Table 1 summarizes some of these assumptions.

First, there is the all or none view of disability. It takes some sensitivity to recognize that blindness comes in degrees, that paralysis is different from one individual to another, and so on. Identification of the nature of the disability and its effects on physical and social events is very crucial to understanding the vocational development of the disabled.

TABLE 1

Assumptions About Career Development Under Ideal Conditions Compared with Under Disabled Conditions

Assumptions about Career Development in the Ideal	Assumptions about Career Development in the Disabled
(1) Career development is systematic.	(1) Career development is unsystematic, influenced by chance (i.e., the disabled better take what they can get).
(2) Career development is psychologically influenced.	(2) Career development is not psychological since the disabled don't have much subjective, psychological life.
(3) Career development is culturally based.	(3) Career development is not important for the disabled.
(4) The total person is involved in career development.	(4) The disability itself overrides the individual's other characteristics in determining career behavior.
(5) People are multipotential regarding careers.	(5) The career options of the disabled are very limited.
(6) Career behavior is developmental.	(6) The career development of the disabled (and the general development as well) is arrested or retarded.
(7) Career development is stressful at choice points.	(7) The career development of the disabled is stressful at all points.

There is also a tendency to see all disability and all disabled persons as being the same. However, such factors as the age of onset of the disability may imply significant differences in adjustment, attitude, and resources of the disabled person in dealing with the disability. A person disabled from birth may grow up dealing with his limitations and in some ways be better able to cope than one injured in maturity. On the other hand, the person disabled later in life may have skills, successes, family, and financial resources to draw upon that the person disabled at a younger age may lack. Such variations in timing of disability have subtle effects on the disabled individual's vocational development.

There is sometimes a tendency for nondisabled observers to blot out the recognition of the psychological, subjective life disabled people experience. Such blotting out helps the nondisabled person avoid thinking uncomfortably about the difficulties the disabled experience in interacting with healthy individuals. However, the price of this comfort for the nondisabled is a tremendous failure to understand the experience of disability and to relate comfortably and effectively with the disabled. Its effects on the disabled person's adjustment to work life is overwhelming, be it stimulated by an employer or professional counselor. One significant effect the attitude has is to lead to the tendency to stereotype the kinds of work that disabled people can do without regard to their individual differences and multipotentiality.

This leads to a related assumption about the work life of the disabled: Disabled people are really very limited in the work they can do and, thus, should be satisfied with whatever they can and are permitted to do. Such thinking allows the justification of the most menial work tasks as appropriate for the disabled in terms of "giving them something to occupy themselves with and earn a living, albeit a modest one."

A final assumption of import often made about the disabled is that development stops after an individual is disabled. The disabled individual's growth is seen as arrested, or at best retarded, and no recognition is displayed of the changing psychological and social needs of disabled individuals as they grow older. Instead of being viewed stereotypically with their age mates, ethnic, or sex groups, the stereotype of disability overrides all others.

When the assumptions about the career development of the disabled are listed as baldly as shown in Table 1, the degree of insensitivity to and lack of understanding of the behavior and subjective lives of disabled people is set in bold relief. While it may be true that some individuals, depending upon the nature of their disability, may be very much the victims of "chance" events in their career lives, in fact, such people are no more buffeted by chance than the nondisabled. In any event, as has been noted elsewhere (Osipow, 1973), the significant events in career behavior and development may well be how the individual responds to vocational stimuli rather than the stimuli themselves. The assumptions that the disabled have little psychological life, that careers are not important to the disabled, and that the development is independent of the disabled individual's overall attributes are clearly not based on careful observation and understanding of disabled individuals.

Thus, while it may be that special attention to the career development of the disabled is necessary and that special concepts applied to them as, for example, has been suggested for the career development of women and for poor black males (Osipow, 1975), numerous points of potential similarity in the forces influencing career behaviors and reactions to those forces between disabled and nondisabled individuals seem to exist.

What Can Be Done? What causes the negative stereotypes? In part, we promote them ourselves by segregation of disabled individuals from society's mainstream, thus reducing the interaction between the disabled and the nondisabled. To some extent, such segregation is being moderated by efforts to make the physical environment more compatible with disability: ramps for wheelchairs, elevators, and modified rest room facilities, for example. These changes not only have the effect of making the environment more hospitable for the disabled and, as a result, increasing the degree of vocational participation possible for disabled people but, in addition, have the very desirable side effect of sensitizing the nondisabled public to disabled people. Such reminders make nondisabled people think more about the disabled as people with distinctive individual characteristics rather than as a stereotyped group to be shut away in a sheltered workshop, or worse.

Counselors and teachers need to develop attitudes and skills in connection with their work of counseling and teaching the disabled; counselors and teachers must learn about their own attitudes toward the disabled and understand how these attitudes affect their counseling and teaching effectiveness with the disabled. More cognitively, the counselor and teacher must learn to differentiate among the disabled, to cope with any negative or guilty feelings possessed toward the disabled, and to recognize the existence of the subjective aspects in the life of the disabled person.

Summary

In this chapter we have reviewed the major concepts of career development theory and the assumptions underlying them. It seems reasonable to conclude that while a considerable dissimilarity between the assumptions about career development in the disabled and nondisabled exists, in fact the career development of the disabled possesses many points of commonality with that of nondisabled people. Efforts to integrate thinking about the disabled into the mainstream of career development research and theory are needed, and greater exposure and explicit discussion of the personality and development of the disabled, and attitudes toward them, seem to be required in counselor and teacher-training programs.

BIBLIOGRAPHY

Ginzberg, E., Ginsburg, S. W., Alexrad, S., and Herma, J. L. *Occupational Choice: An Approach to a General Theory.* New York: Columbia University Press, 1951.

Holland, J. L. "A Theory of Vocational Choice," *Journal of Counseling Psychology,* 1959, 6: 35-45.

Holland, J. L. *The Psychology of Vocational Choice.* Waltham, Mass.: Blaisdell, 1966.

Holland, J. L. *Making Vocational Choices.* Englewood Cliffs, N.J.: Prentice-Hall, 1973.

Osipow, S. H. "What Do We Really Know About Career Development?" in Gysbers, N. and Pritchard, D., eds. *Proceedings of National Conference on Vocational Education.* Columbia, Mo.: University of Missouri, 1969.

Osipow, S. H. *Theories of Career Development,* 2d ed. Englewood Cliffs, N.J.: Prentice-Hall, 1973.

Osipow, S. H. "The Relevance of Theories of Career Development to 'Special Groups': Problems, Needed Data, and Implications," in Picou, S. and Campbell, R. E., Eds. *The Career Behavior of Special Groups.* Columbus, Ohio: Charles E. Merrill, 1975 [in press].

Osipow, S. H. Ed. *Women's Careers: How They Develop.* Columbus, Ohio: Charles E. Merrill, 1975 [in press].

Roe, A. "Early Determinants of Vocational Choice," *Journal of Counseling Psychology,* 1957, 4: 212-217.

Roe, A. and Klos, D. "Occupational Classification," *The Counseling Psychologist,* 1969, 1 (3): 84-92.

Senesh, L. and Osipow, S. H. "Fundamental Ideas of Career Education," in Senesh, L., Ed. *New Paths in Social Science Curriculum Design.* Chicago: Science Research Associates, 1973.

Super, D. E. "A Theory of Vocational Development," *American Psychologist,* 1953, 8: 185-190.

Super, D. E., Starishevsky, R., Matlin, N. and Jordan, J. P. *Career Development: Self-Concept Theory.* New York: CEEB Research Monograph, no. 4, 1963.

Wright, B. A. "Some Psychological Aspects of Disability," in Malikin, D. and Rusalem, H., eds. *Vocational Rehabilitation of the Disabled.* New York: New York University Press, 1969.

IMPLICATIONS FOR REHABILITATION PRACTICE

(1) Rehabilitation workers can be as subject as others to stereotypes about the career development of disabled persons. Such stereotypes predispose the worker to place unwarranted limits upon his client, thus obscuring his essential vocational individuality and constricting his opportunities.

(2) Since disability does not halt vocational development or channel it in a few stereotyped directions (unless we make it so), it is critical for those who serve the disabled to assess their vocational histories and current vocational status in a wholly individualized framework. Experience obtained with other disabled persons who share common characteristics with the current client are not fully useful yardsticks for individual program planning today.

(3) If society is ever to consider disabled persons as individuals rather than members of an artificial class, the process of attitudinal change

will have to start with rehabilitation workers themselves. All too often subtle and covert attitudes and behaviors manifested by the counselor contradict his expressed commitment to individuality and enslave the client to society's misconceptions.

(4) Vocational rehabilitation is still too often viewed as a procedure through which the disabled person is helped to prepare for, enter, and succeed in a job. If a job is all that concerns them, rehabilitation counselors will play a limited role in vocational development. In reality, vocational rehabilitation should be career-oriented and should consider postrehabilitation employment as one event in the total vocational development of the person. This point argues strongly for a lifetime vocational rehabilitation service for many rather than a phenomenological fixation upon early employment after which, in most cases, the rehabilitation curtain falls forever.

CHAPTER IV

ATTITUDES TOWARD DISABILITY

SETTING THE SCENE

Beyond the direct consequences of the disability itself (manifested in pain, discomfort, reduced functioning levels, or incapacity), one of the most limiting aspects of a handicap is the attitudes of self and others toward the disability. Daily experience brings most disabled persons into contact with other people who perceive the handicapping condition and the handicapped person negatively. Such nondisabled individuals consequently adopt rejecting and avoidant behaviors which constrict the life experience and opportunities of the disabled person even further. In personal terms, these behaviors precipitate incalculable suffering and pain and, equally important from the viewpoint of a democratic society, they violate human rights and opportunities as effectively as any authoritarian regime. In practical terms, handicapped people and rehabilitation workers consistently report that the attitudes of the nondisabled as evidenced by their public behaviors often are more limiting than the disability itself.

Over the years, shrewd observers have noted the wide range and inconsistency of attitudes toward the disabled in American society. These experiential findings have been confirmed and extended by an extensive literature on the subject. Unfortunately, attitudes are difficult to measure and are contaminated by innumerable variables in the social setting, resulting in published studies that are methodologically vulnerable. Despite these difficulties, researchers have pressed on toward attaining a more sophisticated understanding of attitudes toward disability because they realize that attitudes play a major role in defining the life experience of most handicapped people.

As yet, however, progress in measurement has yielded few direct benefits to the handicapped. In fact, disabled persons assert that their own daily experiences are by far the most cogent source of evidence concerning bias and rejection in our culture. The individual who suffers profound losses from irrational attitudes sees the problem not so much as one of measurement as of control, modification, and counteraction. Thus, the central questions to be kept in mind in reading the paper that follows are: What have we learned that will help disabled people to cope with negative attitudes? How can we engineer a more equitable and comfortable ecology for the handicapped residents of this country?

CHAPTER IV

ATTITUDES TOWARD DISABILITY

Jerome Siller

Reactions to handicapped people are wide ranging and often quite complex. While certain individuals feel comfortable when interacting with a disabled person, for most this is a salient experience, eliciting anxiety and, in extreme instances, even aversion. Those who experience only mild discomfort with the disabled appear capable or recognizing their sensitivity and humaneness, despite being bothered by a cosmetic or functional condition. Strongly aversive or what may be called "gut" reactions are proportionately rare in the general population; but like most exaggerated phenomena often prove informative in the clarity with which they illustrate trends latent in the more general population, and in suggesting the underlying dynamics for their existence.

Typical "gut" reactors frequently express queasy feelings aroused by the sight of disability and vehemently resist working or socializing with severely handicapped individuals. One consequence of such negative emotionality is to generate avoidance behavior in others, thus depriving the disabled of opportunities for free and open interaction with the larger community. In order to disguise the irrationality of extreme "gut" reactions it becomes necessary for many nondisabled people to see the disabled as functionally incapable and emotionally crippled. Such rationalization legitimizes the avoidance and discriminatory attitudes displayed by so many in the larger society toward the disabled.

For the disabled person each new situation and interaction is fraught with ambiguity in that all manner of reactions may be encountered. While many people tend to think of disabilities in the abstract and to generalize their feelings about them, certain conditions

67

elicit specific reactions (Siller et al., 1967a). For example, a woman with communication difficulties reacted very strongly to the thought of deafness, while people who have problems with control are likely to be particularly distressed by cerebral palsy. Blindness almost invariably is perceived as the most disastrous disability, while obesity, of all things, is treated as if it were a criminal act and often is ranked with socially reprehensible conditions like criminality.

The actual relevance of attitudes for behavior has been called into question in a number of oft-quoted studies and reviews (La Piere, 1934; Kutner, Wilkins, and Yarrow, 1952; Wicker, 1969). They and others found the relationship between attitudes and behavior to be highly complex, and that attitudes are only partial determinants of behavior, along with norms, habits, contexts, and expectations (Calder and Ross, 1973; Kelman, 1974). Consequently, even those individuals with strong aversive reactions toward the disabled might behave differently at different times, sometimes even seemingly accepting of them, while basically clinging to their deep-seated prejudices that destroy the possibility of meaningful interactions.

It is apparent that though the link between attitude and behavior may not be of the stimulus-response type it is still of major importance in affecting the lives of the disabled. One may assume with confidence that negative attitudes toward the disabled represent a real barrier to their filling appropriate roles in society.

In the extensive literature on prejudice it has been shown that a close relationship exists between the components of attitude toward a particular ethnic group and toward other ethnic groups. Those favorable toward one group are likely to favor other groups as well, while people who reveal prejudice toward a single ethnic population also bear bias toward ethnic groups generally. Chesler (1965) found that: "individuals who express ethnocentrism toward racial groups, are also likely to express such attitudes toward religious groups, toward nationality groups, and towards social class divisions ... ethnocentrism is expressed to outgroups in general, rather than to only specific types of outgroups." Chesler also concluded that high ethnocentrism appeared significantly correlated with rejection of the physically disabled.

Many researchers used the Attitude Toward Disabled Persons Scale in determining how people felt about disability. One of the problems created by the ATDP is its lack of a clear referent to the term disability. In addition to learning how people felt about physical conditions the scale also evoked connotations of emotional, social, and cultural possibilities for those using it (Smits, Covine, and Edwards, 1971; Siller, 1966). Even the Siller Scales broadly covered all kinds of physical, emotional and intellectual conditions, raising the question to what extent there might be commonalities and important distinctions among all of these groupings. Interestingly, the differences in defining or delimiting the term disability did not seem to contribute to significant variances in scores obtained on the various disability Scales, leading Smits and his coauthors to infer that the disabled, as a whole, have an outgroup quality that arouses generalized feelings toward them.

Disability, along with any other characteristic that conveys the property of difference, most often is negatively tinged and leads to stigmatization. The literature on deviance, marginality status, exceptionality, and stigma indicates that atypicality usually creates unfavorable social consequences for those so labeled. Even those whose differences are usually regarded as fortunate—the wealthy, the highly creative, the very beautiful, or handsome—encounter unique problems along with the favorable effects of their desired characteristics. Yet difference, per se, does not define a person's psychological position. It is the treatment of this difference by society, the stigmatization and rejection encountered by the disabled, which causes them to feel and act like social deviants (Moriarty, 1974).

Clinical experience suggests that the ability to cope with deviance requires considerable ego strength and personal maturity. Still, as Wright (1960; 1974) noted, the positive coping aspects of the disabled are usually overlooked and only the negative features of their conditions are emphasized. Labeling reinforces negative feelings and stereotypical reactions toward the disabled. When labels are avoided, fewer negative attitudes are expressed by the nondisabled and a greater attention is focused on the degree of adequate functioning of each disabled individual (Jaffe, 1967; Richard, Triandis, and Patterson, 1963). Indeed, as Whiteman and Lukoff (1965) reported, the condition of "blindness" is a more negatively potent concept than is that of "a blind person." In brief, negative reactions toward the disabled or deviant are promoted by many social forces which identify and label persons as deficient and functionally inadequate. To more fully understand the dynamics involved in the formation of negative attitudes it is recommended that rehabilitation professionals learn more about the stimulus variables and situational contexts that apply in given situations (Golin, 1970). Perhaps it is the lack of knowledge of such factors that has limited the effectiveness of attitude change programs.

It is important that the social elements influencing attitudes toward the disabled be supplemented by attention to individual personality dynamics. Strong relationships between personality factors and attitudes toward the disabled largely have not been demonstrated with the exception of alienation and authoritarianism (Noonan, Barry, and David, 1970; Siller et al., 1967a; Yuker et al., 1966). Weaker relationships with measures of anxiety, hostility, locus of control, and other variables have also been reported. However, social and experimental situations demonstrate that behavioral effects do occur in interacting with a disabled person in that the nondisabled person may sit farther away, talk about different things, terminate conversations faster, and twitch more (e.g., Comer and Piliavin, 1972; Farina, Sherman and Allen, 1968; Kleck, Ono and Hastorf, 1966). Such behaviors which have been termed "interaction strain" suggest that despite the paucity of confirmatory evidence from questionnaire-type studies, personality factors do play an important role in the formation of attitudes toward the disabled. Clinical experience in psychoanalytic settings suggests a relationship between attitudes toward deviance and such intrapsychic variables as self and body-image, fear of death, symbolic castration, ego strength, separation anxiety, and narcissism. Specific and unique developmental processes also affect reactions to disability, such as fear of loss of communication skills or sensory damage in persons with fears of isolation, or uncertainty about one's own social acceptance.

Social stigma and simple, negative reinforcement notions seem hardly adequate explanations for strong aversive attitudes toward the disabled. Clinically, it has been found that individuals who fantasize and dream of body deformities project ego-alien and negative self-feelings. Psychoanalytic formulations relating deformity to the projection of unacceptable id impulses—the deformity serves as a traumatic symbol of being unloved—suggest the depth of the problem, as well as therapeutic directions for change. The failure of most research studies, dealing with attitudes toward the disabled to examine such variables, results in an oversimplification of the highly complex relationship between attitudes and personality. Hopefully, as more sophisticated conceptualizations and methodologies are developed research in this area will become more mature and lead to greater clarification and application of new insights related to attitudinal formation.

It can be seen that a full understanding of the dynamics underlying a reaction to the disabled requires recognition of intrapsychic, experiential, and social factors. Outstanding work in this regard has been contributed by the Somatopsychologists in their consideration of such phenomena and concepts as spread, position of the observer, expectation discrepancy, and restriction of environmental opportunities in accord with expectations (e.g., Barker et al., 1953; Dembo, 1969, Wright, 1960, 1974). Thus, Wright (1974) indicates that pity, fear, uneasiness, and guilt lead to negative attitudes while genuine sympathy, respect, appreciation, and warm interpersonal relationships are connected with positive ones.

The disabled person's own reactions to his condition can serve as a stimulus affecting responses to him. In early stages of disablement such reactions as anxiety, depression, grief, mourning, denial, and regressive forms of behavior, and later long-term modes of adjustment, such as passivity, dependency, aggressivity, withdrawal, compensation, and coping mechanisms, will be important determinants of how the nondisabled will respond to his disability (Siller, in Meislin, in press).

The nature of measurement of attitudes toward the disabled presents difficulties due to the varying methodologies employed and basic assumptions made. Very few systematic and extended programs of study have been conducted in the past. If attitudes toward the disabled are measured along a single dimension of positiveness-negativeness (e.g., the Attitude Toward Disabled Persons Scale of Yuker, Block, & Young, 1966) one might obtain different results than if using an approach measuring several dimensions of attitude (Siller *et al.,* 1967a, b; Siller, 1970). Most of the single score measures seem to tap a mixture of dimensions on primarily an affective (feeling) level. Multidimensional scales such as those developed by the writer and his associates and confirmed by others (e.g., Kohler and Graves, 1973) have the advantage of measuring both affect and other types of attitude dimensions as well. As one moves from uni- to multidimensional reasoning, different issues become important.

Considerable information has been obtained through the increasing recognition of the importance of multidimensional approaches regarding attitudes toward the disabled (Jordan, 1968; Whiteman and Lukoff, 1964, 1965). Major theoretical issues of the dimensionality of this attitude domain were empirically investigated in a series of studies under the writer's direction (Ferguson, 1970; Siller, 1970; Siller et al., 1967a, b; Vann, 1970). Using factor analytic procedures on sets of attitude questionnaires dealing with a variety of disability conditions seven major attitude components were identified. These were:

(1) *Interaction Strain*—uneasiness in the presence of disabled persons and uncertainty as how to deal with them.

(2) *Rejection of Intimacy*—rejection of close, particularly familial, relationships with the disabled.

(3) *Generalized Rejection*—a pervasive negative and derogatory approach to disabled persons with consequent advocacy of segregation.

(4) *Authoritarian Virtuousness*—ostensibly a "prodisabled" orientation, this factor is really rooted in an authoritarian context which manifests itself in a call for special treatment that is less benevolent and more harmful than it seems.

(5) *Inferred Emotional Consequences*—intense hostile references to the character and emotions of the disabled person.

(6) *Distressed Identification*—personalized hypersensitivity to disabled persons who serve as activators of anxiety about one's own vulnerability to disability.

(7) *Imputed Functional Limitations*—devaluation of the capacities of a disabled person in coping with his environment.

The seven dimensions are fairly comprehensive in describing the attitude domain for a wide range of conditions, amputation, blindness, cancer, cosmetic disfigurement, deafness, and obesity. While these attitude components generalize from one disability to another, some attitude components which are specific for certain disabilities only also occur. Individual scales for each disability condition have been constructed by Siller and his associates which can be used to measure the components of attitude identified. Additionally, a general or cross-disability measure also is available.

Following a factorial approach, Siller engaged in a study of the components that help to explain important aspects of attitudes toward disabled persons. It was found that:

(1) Salient dimensions of attitude toward the disabled can be

identified and measured. The seven described above can represent an initial taxonomy in this direction.

(2) There is a high degree of generality of attitude components across disabilities. An attitude component identified for one disability, unless very specific for that condition, likely will occur for other conditions.

(3) Components of attitude within a disability tend to be positively correlated. Thus an individual who is positive (or negative) in regard to one component will likely be positive (or negative) in regard to the other components. Further, a person who is favorably or unfavorably inclined toward one disability will tend to be similarly inclined toward other disabilities. Greatest consistencies in attitudes across disabilities ordinarily will be on the same component, for example, Generalized Rejection on amputation with Generalized Rejection on blindness.

(4) Age, sex, and other demographic variables are important mostly in the manner in which attitudes toward the disabled are expressed rather than in their formation. Thus, women may have attitudes similar to men but will be more likely to express them in ways influenced by their sex role. Adolescents of both sexes tend to be more rejecting than are younger or older persons, and persons better educated tend to be most accepting. Personal contact with the disabled may either substantially improve or worsen attitudes depending upon the quality of the previous interaction. Ethnicity (Richardson et al., 1961) and cultural bias (Jaques et al., 1970; Jordan, 1968) may also be implicated in reactions to the disabled. It is very difficult to make hard generalizations regarding the influence of these various demographic factors as their operations are complex and unlikely to be described in a direct and simple way.

(5) The attitudinal components of interaction strain, rejection of intimacy, generalized rejection, inferred emotional consequences, and impaired functional limitations are readily recognized by persons holding them. These five tend to be correlated with each other and readily can be seen as an affective or "general" cluster. Distressed identification, on the other hand, while also affectively charged, tends to support repressive mechanisms and blocking in the minds of persons. Unlike all of the others, authoritarian virtuousness, which

correlates with alienation, dogmatism, and authoritarianism, is unlikely to be perceived subjectively and accurately. Those holding this attitude to any great extent are likely to have subordinating styles that would be particularly damaging for individuals desiring to work with the disabled.

A number of significant, general conclusions for rehabilitation workers are suggested by a review of the literature on attitudes toward the disabled. Considering the importance of this issue, the amount of work done is surprisingly little and much of the research is methodologically flawed. However, some of the more firm conclusions are worth noting:

(1)   The presence of a deviance severely impairs vocational and social possibilities. Job hiring practices mostly are determined by individuals who often reflect society's rejecting attitudes, rather than by deliberate, clearly stated company policies. When systematic hiring of the disabled is enforced, most of the anticipated problems never arise.

(2)   Like almost everyone else, rehabilitation workers value youth, health, beauty, and brightness, characteristics which may be less common in disability groups. The gravity and pessimistic prognoses of many conditions inhibit involvement and interest on the part of many professionals. This is reflected by a reluctance to work with certain types of disabled persons as a career choice. Additionally, many upward striving middle class professionals are more comfortable with clients who share their own value and cultural systems than with the increasing number of rehabilitation clients who come from disadvantaged and culturally different backgrounds.

(3)   To date, significant progress in changing attitudes toward the disabled has not been achieved. Attitude change programs attempt to manipulate increased social contacts by means of informational campaigns. Contact interventions may run the hazard of strengthening and reinforcing negative attitudes rather than fostering more positive ones. The quality rather than just the quantity of such contacts must be carefully controlled. Providing information to selected target groups in itself seems quite futile. Sands and Zalkind (1972) attempted to

change employers' attitudes toward epilepsy through the medium of a high powered educational campaign that failed despite the seeming excellence of the program itself. Anthony (1972), summarizing the literature on changing social attitudes toward the mentally, physically, and intellectually handicapped, concluded that either information or contact alone is insufficient to have a favorable impact, but that a combination of the two offered significantly and consistently might influence attitudes favorably.

(4) Attitude change toward the disabled likely will be most successful when efforts are directed to the affective state of the nondisabled person (i.e., the "gut" level) in a meaningful way. For example, Blank (1954) indicated that disturbed attitudes and behaviors of the professional worker with the disabled could be reduced through analysis of their countertransference behaviors (emotional reactions of the professional based upon unconscious factors), without the necessity of an extensive treatment program. One must recognize that some persons will require major psychodynamic changes, but even "intractable" persons can be somewhat desensitized, particularly when helped by the disabled person.

(5) This writer believes that it is the responsibility of the people most affected—the disabled themselves—to shape their relationships with the nondisabled so as to maximize successful interactions (Siller et al., 1967a). To this end social coping skills should be part of any rehabilitation program. Rehabilitants, as well as the professional workers, should be taught a specific repertoire of skills and strategies for handling such basic issues as curiosity about disabling conditions, offers of help, and initial interpersonal encounters. The dimensions of attitude formation, developed by the writer and others described above, would be of great assistance in formulating and evaluating such a training program. The writings of Davis (1961), Dembo (1969), and Wright (1960), to mention but a few, also offer much that could be used in training programs.

Summary

The importance of attitudes toward the disabled has been discussed in a number of contexts. Some of the implications of particular meaning for rehabilitation workers might be summarized as follows:

(1) Attitudes toward the disabled are highly varied, but more frequently negative. Strongly aversive feelings, though proportionately small, disproportionally influence the larger society.

(2) Continuities exist among attitudes toward various social, cultural, emotional, intellectual, and physically based deviancies. At least on the level of stereotype, disabilities may be lumped together as belonging to a common unit.

(3) The perception of difference usually leads to an individual being considered deviant and results in stigmatization.

(4) Rather than responding to the individual qualities and competencies of disabled persons, nondisabled people tend to label and consequently stereotype them, with untoward consequences for the disabled person and society. Any steps that promote individualization in dealing with disabled persons can help to break down negative stereotypes.

(5) The prevalence and pervasiveness of negative attitudes toward the disabled suggest that social, cultural, and psychodynamic factors all operate. Psychological problems of the nondisabled may be acted out in relation to the disabled, and it would be well for the disabled to be aware of this possibility so they may be spared inappropriate self-references.

(6) Simplistic unidimensional considerations of attitudes toward the disabled are being supplanted by an appreciation of the multidimensional nature of the problem. An initial taxonomy of salient dimensions of attitude toward the disabled has been described that brings together what might otherwise appear to be very disparate phenomena. These attitudinal components also can serve as elements in educational programs for the disabled, rehabilitation personnel, and family members.

(7) The results of attitude change programs with the general public have thus far not been particularly fruitful. Direct training of

disabled persons to effectively deal with their interpersonal environment through the acquisition of social coping skills offers hope for immediate improvement. As was found in a wide variety of self-help programs, the mere act of doing something about one's own condition is of itself therapeutic and the beginning of change.

BIBLIOGRAPHY

Anthony, W. A. "Societal Rehabilitation: Changing Society's Attitudes Toward the Physically and Mentally Disabled," *Rehabilitation Psychology,* 1972, 19, 117-126.

Barker, R. G., Wright, B. A., Meyerson, L., and Gonick, M. R. *Adjustment to Physical Handicap and Illness: A Survey of the Social Psychology of Physique and Disability.* Bulletin 55. New York: Social Science Research Council, 1953.

Blank, H. R. "Countertransference Problems in the Professional Worker. *The New Outlook for the Blind,"* 1954, 48, 185-188.

Calder, B. J. and Ross, M. "Attitudes and Behavior," *General Learning Corporation,* 1973.

Chesler, M. A. "Ethnocentrism and Attitudes Toward the Physically Disabled." *Journal of Personality and Social Psychology,* 1965, 2, 877-882.

Comer, R. J. and Piliavin, J. A. "The Effects of Physical Deviance Upon Face-to-Face Interaction: The Other Side," *Journal of Personality and Social Psychology,* 1972, 23, 33-39.

Davis, F. "Deviance Disavowal: The Management of Strained Interaction by the Visibly Handicapped," *Social Problems,* 1961, 9, 120-132.

Dembo, T. "Rehabilitation Psychology and Its Immediate Future: A Problem of Utilization of Psychological Knowledge," *Psychological Aspects of Disability,* 1969, 16, 63-72.

Farina, A., Sherman, M., and Allen, J. G. "Role of Physical Abnormalities in Interpersonal Perception and Behavior," *Journal of Abnormal Psychology,* 1968, 73, 590-593.

Ferguson, L. T. "Components of Attitudes Toward the Deaf," *Proceedings of the 78th Annual Convention of the American Psychological Association,* 1970, 5, 693-694.

Golin, A. K. "Stimulus Variables in the Measurement of Attitudes Toward Disability," *Rehabilitation Counseling Bulletin,* 1970, 14, 20-26.

Jaffe, J. "What's in a Name—Attitudes Toward Disabled Persons," *Personnel and Guidance Journal,* 1967, 46, 375-381.

Jaques, M. E., Linkowski, D. C., and Sieka, F. L. "Cultural Attitudes Toward Disability: Denmark, Greece, and the United States," *International Journal of Social Psychiatry,* 1970, 16, 54-62.

Jordan, J. E. *Attitudes Toward Education and Physically Disabled Persons in Eleven Nations.* Latin American Studies Center, Michigan State University, 1968.

Kleck, R., Ono, H., and Hastorf, A. H. "The Effects of Physical Deviance Upon Face-To-Face Interaction," *Human Relations,* 1966, 19, 425-436.

Kelman, H. C. Attitudes Are Alive and Well and Gainfully Employed in the Sphere of Action. *American Psychologist,* 1974, 29, 310-24.

Kohler, E. T. and Graves, W. H. III. "Factor Analysis of the Disability Factor Scales with the Little Jiffy, Mark III," *Rehabilitation Psychology,* 1973, 20, 102-107.

Kutner, B., Wilkins, C., and Yarrow, P. R. "Verbal Attitudes and Overt Behavior Involving Racial Prejudice," *Journal of Abnormal and Social Psychology,* 1952, 47, 649-652.

LaPiere, R. T. "Attitudes Versus Actions," *Social Forces,* 1934, 13, 230-237.

Moriarity, T. "Role of Stigma in the Experience of Deviance," *Journal of Personality and Social Psychology,* 1974, 6, 849-855.

Noonan, J. R., Barry, J. R., and Davis, H. C. "Personality Determinants in Attitudes Toward Visible Disability," *Journal of Personality,* 1970, 38, 1-15.

Richardson, S. A., Goodman, N., Hastorf, A. H., and Dornbusch, S. M. "Cultural Uniformity in Reaction to Physical Disabilities," *American Sociological Review,* 1961, 26, 341-347.

Rickard, T. E., Triandis, H. C., and Patterson, C. H. "Indices of Employer Prejudice Toward Disabled Applicants," *Journal of Applied Psychology,* 1963, 47, 52-55.

Sands, H. and Zalkind, S. S. "Effects of an Educational Campaign To Change Employer Attitudes Toward Hiring Epileptics," *Epilepsia,* 1972, 13, 87-96.

Siller, J. *Conceptual and Methodological Issues in the Study of Attitudes Toward Disability.* Presented at the American Personnel and Guidance Association Annual Convention, 1966.

Siller, J. "The Generality of Attitudes Toward the Disabled," *Proceedings of the 78th Annual Convention of the American Psychological Association,* 1970, 5, 697-698.

Siller, J. "Psychosocial Aspects of Disability," in J. Meislin (Ed.), *Rehabilitation Medicine and Psychiatry.* Springfield, Ill.: C. C. Thomas, in press.

Siller, J., Chipman, A., Ferguson, L. T., and Vann, D. H. "Attitudes of the Nondisabled Toward the Physically Disabled," *Studies in Reactions to Disability: XI.* New York: School of Education, New York University, 1967a.

Siller, J., Ferguson, L. T., Vann, D. H., and Holland, B. "Structure of Attitudes Toward the Physically Disabled," *Studies in Reactions to Disability: XII.* New York: School of Education, New York University, 1967b.

Smits, S. J., Conine, T. A., and Edwards, L. D. "Definitions of Disability as Determinants of Scores on the Attitude Toward Disabled Persons Scale," *Rehabilitation Counseling Bulletin,* 1971, 15, 227-235.

Vann, D. H. "Components of Attitudes Toward the Obese Including Presumed Responsibility for the Condition," *Proceedings of the 78th Annual Convention of the American Psychological Association,* 1970, 5, 695-696.

Whiteman, M. and Lukoff, I. F. "A Factorial Study of Sighted People's Attitudes Toward Blindness," *Journal of Social Psychology,* 1964, 64, 339-353.

Whiteman, M. and Lukoff, I. F. "Attitudes Toward Blindness and Other Physical Handicaps," *Journal of Social Psychology,* 1965, 66, 125-145.

Wicker, A. W. "Attitudes Versus Actions: The Relationship of Verbal and Overt Behavioral Responses to Attitude Objects," *Journal of Social Issues,* 1969, 25, 41-78.

Wright, B. A. *Physical Disability—a Psychological Approach.* New York: Harper & Row, 1960.

Wright, B. A. "An Analysis of Attitudes—Dynamics and Effects," *The New Outlook for the Blind,* 1974, 108-118.

Yuker, H. E., Block, J. R., and Younng, J. H. *The Measurement of Attitudes toward Disabled Persons.* Albertson, New York: Human Resources Center, 1966.

IMPLICATIONS FOR REHABILITATION PRACTICE

Rehabilitation workers spend much time deploring negative attitudes toward handicapped persons but engage in little organized action to modify these attitudes. As Siller suggests, clinical experience and research evidence confirm the presence of differential attitudes toward disability, in general, and specific disabilities, in particular. The evolution of more precise means of assessing attitudes has now reached the point where measurement for measurement's sake is unwarranted. Constructive action to cope with negative attitudes should become an integral part of the rehabilitation process. Unfortunately, as Siller indicates, the traditional efforts undertaken in this direction (educating the nondisabled and increasing the degree of contact between the two groups) have not solved the problem. Despite everything we have done thus far, negative attitudes continue to constitute dominant constrictors of opportunities for severely handicapped persons.

As a clinician, as well as a researcher, Siller suggests an additional means through which disabled persons may be liberated from the inhibiting effects of negative public attitudes—that of training the object of these attitudes (disabled individuals) to cope more effectively with them and to serve as a change agent in the course of their social contacts in the community. This idea should lead to the development of structured formal rehabilitation training programs which systematically instruct the handicapped in techniques of managing the attitudes of self and others toward disability. For much too long, we have taken essential areas of human endeavor for granted in the belief that somehow handicapped persons would master the requisite skills required and knowledges. Time and again, however, it has been demonstrated that many disabled clients do not learn such skills automatically in the course of everyday interactions. And, so it is with attitudes. Along with everything else that should be done legislatively, judicially, and educationally to reshape attitudes, experiments should be undertaken to teach handicapped persons to be effective shapers of public attitudes toward them. Not only will this bring a new source of human power into the attitude modification picture, but it will give the disabled persons greater responsibility for managing their own lives and the terms under which they are to live. Also, even the attempt to improve one's life situation is ego building and adds to a sense of fulfillment.

PART II

REHABILITATION PRACTICE

CHAPTER V

THE CONSUMER AND THE REHABILITATION PROCESS

SETTING THE SCENE

Client conformity and compliance have long been valued by many rehabilitation workers as favorable signs in the rehabilitation process. Ideal client behavior still is perceived by some rehabilitators in terms of readiness to accept counselor decisions without equivocation and a capacity for postponing current satisfactions in order to achieve long-term employment goals. The "good" or the "cooperative" clients often are perceived as ones who place themselves unquestioningly in the hands of their counselors and respond positively to every nuance of counselor guidance. Indeed, counselor voices are still heard in professional agency corridors mourning the decreasing frequency of the "goal-oriented," acquiescent disabled people in their caseloads, suggesting that some insidious process is taking place in society which is generating more resistant and questioning client behaviors.

A combination of social forces, including the recruitment of disabled persons from the inner city (where compliance with the establishment is less common) and the growing awareness and strength of the rehabilitation consumer movement throughout the land, definitely is bringing larger contingents of more aggressive disabled individuals into rehabilitation agency offices. Encouraged by the human rights victories of the 1960s, these clients do not consider themselves to be the clay out of which rehabilitation workers can mold desirable products. On the contrary, they are disputing our solutions to some of the fundamental problems of rehabilitation, such as what the relationship should be between rehabilitation clients and counselors, where the locus of rehabilitation decision-making should lie, and how rehabilitation services should be delivered to disabled persons. In practical terms, consumerism is becoming one of the emerging forces that will shape the rehabilitation process of tomorrow, affecting every professional and lay participant. Although the role of the consumer is a critical issue for many counselors, the ultimate resolution of the

matter may well lie in the collective views of consumers themselves. As rehabilitation clients begin to express themselves more
fully and as they seek added strength through self-help organizations, their voices are likely to become more decisive in determining the course of rehabilitation in the future. It is for this reason
that the editors decided to include a chapter in this book that
reflects client viewpoints and indicates the manner in which such
viewpoints may influence everyday rehabilitation practice in the
years ahead.

CHAPTER V

THE CONSUMER AND THE REHABILITATION PROCESS

Lila Rosenblum and Herbert Rusalem

When a disabled person approaches a rehabilitation agency for assistance he is usually met with a show of interest, concern, respect, and even compassion. However, in the process of setting up appointments for medical and psychological counseling as well as other services, as part of a large caseload, and in the midst of a bustling office, the client often begins to feel as if he is being treated as an object rather than as a person. Things are done to and for him and, despite efforts to keep him informed about what is happening, he finds himself assigned to the role of an observer at his own rehabilitation. This is not a recent development, Wright (1960), some 15 years ago, proposing that the client be considered a comanager of his own program rather than as a spectator "visiting" an agency for a "reshaping" job by experts. Not infrequently, clients contribute little to their programs, sometimes making only one major decision, whether or not to participate in the process.

Although the degree of such professional or paraprofessional manipulation varies from situation to situation, the traditional approach has been for the client to be treated much like a busy physician treats his patients. As in the doctor-patient relationship, rehabilitation counselors frequently view themselves as superordinates who are armed with specialized knowledge, skills, and attitudes that enable them to proceed as they see fit. In contradistinction, disabled individuals tend to be viewed as relatively helpless, confused, and troubled persons who are unable to mobilize themselves and contribute meaningfully to their rehabilitation. In essence the rehabilitation relationship often seems one between a defenseless child and a wise and protective parent.

For the first 40 or so years of its existence, the perception of clients as recipients of bounty by the rehabilitation movement seemed consistent with the prevailing attitudes of the larger society. "Charity"-receiving clients were expected to accept their lower status, while rehabilitation professionals were expected to thrive on their transcending position. In the middle and late 1960s, however, the winds of change began to blow, not only in rehabilitation but in all the human services. For the first time, the objects of the helping process, the consumers, began to raise questions about their subordinate status and, concluding that there were many demeaning elements in the typical helping process, some began to organize into action-oriented groups whose major purpose was to place the disadvantaged individual in a more favorable position to negotiate with society's institutions and gatekeepers.

In rehabilitation, this movement found root among young disabled college students and college-trained adults for whom secondary citizenship and patronizing attitudes were especially abhorrent. Groups like the Disabled-in-Action in New York City surfaced and demanded an altered rehabilitation environment. The motivating force behind this development was the belief that disabled persons should participate more fully in decisions made about them, both as individuals and as a social group. Among their complaints were:

(1) Vital community and agency decisions about rehabilitation policies and procedures are being made without sufficient input from disabled persons.

(2) The disabled client rarely functions as an equal on the rehabilitation team.

(3) Professional and paraprofessional attitudes toward the disabled more nearly reflect those of the nondisabled majority than of the disabled themselves.

(4) Rehabilitation workers are not performing adequately as advocates of the disabled in the community.

(5) Although well-meant, recent efforts to enhance the participation of rehabilitation consumers in relevant matters have largely appeared a form of tokenism.

The philosophical underpinnings of the rehabilitation consumer awakening can be found in the basic concepts of American democracy, neighborliness, fairness, and mutual respect. These constructs seem self-evident, but it has been a characteristic of American society that verbalizations about our values extend far beyond our everyday behaviors. Thus, it is in the American tradition that clients work to close the gap between expressed ideals, and far from ideal practices in the rehabilitation establishment. One of the contradictions between promise and practice is seen in the frequency with which the Rogerian belief of self-direction is cited by counselors, and the few times that clients are actually permitted to be self-directing. Another example can be found in our claim that we attempt to rehabilitate clients according to their fullest potential, but then offer them the first (and often easiest) job available, often well below their potential. Still another example is the rehabilitation agency that presses colleges and employers to extend educational and employment opportunities for severely disabled clients, but then fail to employ qualified clients as staff members. It appears evident that the rehabilitation establishment has much unfinished business in becoming more genuine, and that the problem of consumer satisfaction with his role in the process will be a focus of concern for years to come.

It is revealing that the complaints of the rehabilitation consumer have received scant attention from rehabilitation personnel. One of the landmarks in rectifying this condition was a meeting of rehabilitation workers and consumers conducted in 1973 at Bloomington, Minnesota, under the sponsorship of Mankato State College. The central purpose of this meeting was to establish lines of communication between rehabilitation workers and rehabilitation consumers and to provide a forum in which clients could present personal perceptions of their rehabilitation experiences. In the context of this free and constructive interchange of views, consumers offered the following observations (among others):

(1) Rehabilitation counselors tend to be cold and impersonal and provide insufficient help with personal problems.
(2) Rehabilitation workers do not have adequate specialized knowledge and skill to deal with certain less familiar disabilities.

(3) Rehabilitation training and placement is more often deter-
      mined by counselor perceptions of labor market conditions
      than by the disabled person's vocational potential.
(4) Some forms of employment for the disabled (especially in
      sheltered workshops) are demeaning.

The report of this conference (Drake, 1973) indicated that participating rehabilitation agency staff members considered the meetings to
be an extremely important and helpful development. ". . . The client is
no longer passive, if he ever was. He is not passive about saying what he
thinks is wrong, but he also is not passive about wanting to 'get into the
act' to improve things."

Rehabilitation leaders are beginning to discuss the client-
consumer's role more openly and aggressively. As an example, Gellman
(1974) noted:

> Virtually everywhere in the rehabilitation world, there is a grow-
> ing call for consumer involvement. . . . The handicapped and
> their advocates are asking for participation in decisions affecting
> the allocation of funds. . . . Physically disabled persons are playing
> a more active role in determining their treatment and are begin-
> ning to participate in setting goals for their own rehabilitation
> and in evaluating the results.

From a sheltered workshop administrator's viewpoint, Barton
(1972) reported his perceptions of what a composite client might say to
the person who serves him, if given an opportunity to do so: "Listen,
rehabilitation workers. Treat me as a person not as a diagnostic label, a
typical client, or an object of a service contract. . . . When you talk of
my rehabilitation plan it cannot be *my* plan if I have no say as to its
goals and the means for achieving them."

For many years, rehabilitation clients have written about their service experiences, sometimes with bitterness and dissatisfaction. For
example, Chevigny pointedly accused the agencies for the blind, where
he had sought help, of attempting to psychologically impoverish him,
making few efforts to view him as an individual with special talents
and interests. Since the disabled authors who write about their rehabilitation experiences may not be representative of rehabilitation
clients as a whole, it is difficult to generalize from their presentations.

Suffice it to say that there appears to be a group of severely disabled persons with evident talents and advantages who found the rehabilitation process to be unsuitable for them, and, in some cases, even destructive. Indeed, as one reviews the self-reports of the disabled authors of books describing the processes they used to master their handicapping conditions, one is struck by how little of the credit for their success they attribute to formal rehabilitation programs and how much of it they give to their own resources and the assistance they received from certain significant people in their lives. A few behavioral scientists have examined the rehabilitation process to ascertain its meaning to clients. Scott did so in relation to rehabilitation services for blind persons and concluded that the agencies he studied did not necessarily exemplify positive and constructive approaches to the problems generated by this disability.

It ought to be a matter of pride to rehabilitation workers that organizations of handicapped persons have taken the initiative to press for improved services since this would seem to be a confirmation of rehabilitation's long-stated view that disabled individuals can manage their own affairs. Yet, activist groups of disabled persons often arouse anxiety on the part of rehabilitation personnel and, sometimes, they even precipitate avoidant reactions among administrators and clinicians. Not infrequently, collective action by disabled persons is in response to the failure of professionals to represent them adequately. In any event, the outcomes of such social action are almost always psychosocially favorable in that the victories achieved provide disabled persons with a sense of augmented individual and group self-worth and a feeling that they can influence the course of events. In discussing self-help groups, Zola (1973) observed:

It is not accidental that major changes in the architecture of public buildings have been pushed by paraplegics, reduction of drug maintenance costs by "mended hearts," extension of medicare coverage by ostomates, new speech therapies by laryngectomees, or a new profession, enterostomal therapy, largely created and staffed by former patients. . . . No matter how sophisticated, tolerant, or even understanding the unafflicted become, the sufferers will ultimately have to see to their own needs by banding together and pushing.

As part of a pioneering investigation (Vineberg, 1973), disabled individuals were interviewed at the Texas Institute for Rehabilitation and Research in July 1968 about their perceptions of the rehabilitation process. One of the central findings emerging from this study was that patients and former patients did not see the discreet professional disciplines (for example, medicine, psychology, rehabilitation counseling, and physical therapy) in the same way that rehabilitation specialists see themselves. This finding suggests that communication between a rehabilitation agency and its clientele can be so limited that patients are not certain about who does what to whom and how they should relate to the various members of the rehabilitation team.

In a pilot study conducted at the Speech and Hearing Institute in New York City, clients were asked to present their perceptions of their rehabilitation experiences. The trends in these findings were:

(1)   Clients view rehabilitation as a fragmented process rather than the integrated and comprehensive experience their rehabilitation workers perceive it to be.

(2)   Movement from one agency to the next as part of a total rehabilitation plan is not perceived by clients as an orderly or even necessary progression.

(3)   The counselor's role was not perceived by these clients as being central. More commonly, these disabled persons attributed their progress to the rehabilitation team or to their own efforts.

(4)   There was a tendency to view rehabilitation counselors (especially those working for a state agency) as rather mechanistic, formal, and inaccessible.

(5)   Voluntary agency counselors were viewed by the members of this small sample in relatively positive terms. On the other hand, state rehabilitation agency counselors were seen by their clients primarily as authorizers of service.

(6)   Despite the gains that they evidently achieved through rehabilitation in self-confidence, self-respect, self-worth, adjustment to the disability, employment, and sharing in a group experience, these client respondents felt that their potential had not been adequately assessed, that they had not received sufficient supportive counseling, and that they had not been given access to the training that they really wanted or needed.

One of the turning points in the consumer movement occurred in July 1969, when the Social and Rehabilitation Service of the U.S. Department of Health, Education, and Welfare sponsored a National Citizens Conference in Washington, D.C. The Conference Report cogently describes the motivations of the diversified participating individuals and groups:

> They came because they were deeply disturbed about the indifference, the dehumanization, the isolation which has come to permeate our society, making life intolerable for some, unsatisfying for many. . . . The Conference offered an unprecedented opportunity for members of the "power structure" of our society to meet with a cross-section of all America and gain a better understanding of the pressures for making drastic changes in many of the programs and policies which they control.

In summing up the Conference, W. Scott Allan noted some of the common threads that were woven into the discussions. It should be noted that many of these ideas originated with the rehabilitation consumers who participated in the meetings:

(1)   Current services to people are ineffective in scope, character, and organization.

(2)   More consumer involvement in planning and programming is needed in determining needs, planning and administering programs, helping to provide services, and in program evaluation and follow-up.

(3)   Rehabilitation can be made a suitable experience for *both* the disabled and the disadvantaged since these groups have much in common.

(4)   Current major rehabilitation problems exist in the areas of communication, transportation, and public attitudes.

(5)   Both consumers and rehabilitation workers are not legislatively and politically sophisticated and until they become so, there will be problems in obtaining adequate funds for the support of the rehabilitation movement.

Perhaps the most revealing and significant outcome of this meeting

was in the sense of the consumer resolution which was adopted at the
conference:

> ... One of the major defects of HEW—funded programs con-
> sists of failure to provide legal, recognized procedures whereby the
> interests, beliefs, and needs of consumers can be presented as a
> matter of right in rehabilitation policy-making, planning, and
> programming.

Consequently, the Conference recommended legal procedures for obtaining fuller consumer involvement in rehabilitation agencies and
disabled persons. Beyond such legal provisions, the Conference went
on record as urging public and private rehabilitation agencies to take
steps voluntarily to incorporate appropriate consumer representation
in their activities.

The foregoing suggests that the consumer has increasingly become a
focus of political and social concern in the United States, facilitated to
some degree, perhaps, by the pressures exerted on the rehabilitation
establishment by organized groups of disabled individuals. Thus far,
unfortunately, oratory has not been matched by accomplishments.
Today, the ideal of consumer participation in the planning and delivery of rehabilitation services is more firmly established ideationally
than operationally. There is little evidence as yet that this ideal is
approaching realization. The minimal accomplishment thus far has
been fragmented, at best suggesting a token effort and expedient con-
cession rather than wholehearted commitment to the implementation
of the principle. Perhaps the next move toward fuller realization of the
concept will occur when, and if, organizations of disabled persons
achieve a higher degree of unity and militancy so that they can demand early translation of verbal acquiescence into actual everyday
practice. The part that rehabilitation workers should play in this
movement is open to wide discussion. In the past, we have stood on the
sidelines and kept our political skirts clean. It is doubtful if disabled
persons will continue to phlegmatically accept a passive role indefinitely. It is more characteristic of dynamic minority organizations to
feel that either a group is for them or against them in their fight
against social oppression. Some day soon, the rehabilitation movement
will find itself at a crossroads, at which time it will have to decide what
it shall be.

In the meantime, an equally crucial, but long-neglected issue is rising to meet us. That is, what should be the role of the individual consumer in his or her rehabilitation experience? Currently, the rehabilitation process in many agencies relegates the disabled individual to a secondary role in decision-making, goal-setting, and program planning. He is evaluated, counseled, trained, and placed in the framework of a professional's theory, constructs, preferences, or inclinations. In practice, rarely are clients asked for their views about the type of counseling, training, physical and mental restoration, or employment which should be provided. Regardless of the merits of the argument that clients are too troubled to make that decision, or that they lack the knowledge or expertise to resolve such vital issues, or that their objectivity is wanting, the outcome is that we "lay hands" on individuals and mold them in accordance with our perception of what would be right for them. To all intents and purposes, they are like machines and we are the operators.

Viewpoints vary concerning the impact of this manipulative approach on the rehabilitation consumer, but it is hard to see how our taking over vast segments of his or her life can contribute to independence. On the contrary, it can well be argued that such approaches cultivate excessive reliance on others, a phenomenon frequently observed in the medical model in which the patient is required to assume a passive, dependent role. Regardless of other benefits that may be claimed for this counselor-centered diagnosis and treatment model, it is not likely to foster the clients' potential for creative and self-determining activities.

If, indeed, a principal goal of rehabilitation is that of augmenting client independence, one way of maximizing consumer involvement in the rehabilitation process might be that of creating a system whereby clients purchase their own services with vouchers or grants. After learning what they need to become rehabilitated and about available resources, clients play a major role in their rehabilitation program by selecting their service facility and the medical, psychological, or any other types of assistance deemed necessary by their counselor and them for their rehabilitation. Thus, if an agency's or a professional's performance falls below expectations or desires, clients have the option of withdrawing their "business" and taking it elsewhere. Consumers with purchasing power soon find themselves in a relationship that offers them dignity and a greater concern for their need satisfaction. Obviously, there would be problems in such a system, especially in the case of clients who are less capable of making informed choices, but with the development of procedural safeguards, these could be minimized.

Another suggestion is the adoption of an ombundsman arrangement through which counselors or other experienced individuals would be designated to attend to client complaints and assist in resolving client-agency conflicts. At present many counselors would like to perceive themselves as client advocates, but find themselves rendered ineffective when the very organization that pays their salaries is also the one that is allegedly mishandling client interests. Thus, effective ombundsmen would have to be supported independently and without owing loyalty to any specific agency or institution.

A final concern relating the consumers' role during their rehabilitation process centers about counselor training programs. Insufficient attention is paid to rehabilitation consumer rights in the typical university curriculum. In fact, it may be that during a counselor's two-year graduate program not more than a few moments, let alone a class session, is devoted to discussing the current status of consumerism in rehabilitation. By this very neglect, counselor educators may be unconsciously reinforcing trainees' authoritarian tendencies. Added to this is the typical supervisor-trainee relationship during the student's internship. In this relationship trainees are frequently made to feel helpless and inadequate, setting an unfortunate model for future client-counselor interaction. Counselor educators can make a noteworthy contribution to the consumer movement by stressing to their students that human values are more important than procedures and techniques in serving disabled individuals.

BIBLIOGRAPHY

Barton, H. Jr., "Talk *with* Me!," *Journal of Rehabilitation,* 1972, 38: 6, 33.

Chevigny, H., *My Eyes Have a Cold Nose,* New Haven: Yale University Press, 1946

Drake, J., "Minnesota's Consumer Advisory Project," *Rehabilitation Record,* 1973, 14: 2, 25-27.

Gellman, W., "Projections in the Field of Physical Disability." *Rehabilitation Literature,* 1974, 35: 1, 7.

Lewis, S., "The Handicapped Consumer-Professional Speaks," *Journal of Rehabilitation,* 40: 2, 24-25.

U.S. Department of Health, Education, and Welfare. Social and Rehabilitation Service, "People Power: A Report of the Conference." (Washington, D.C.: U.S. Government Printing Office, 1969.)

Vineberg, E., "The Environment as a Network of Judgments Regarding Staff Roles," *Archives of Physical Medicine and Rehabilitation,* 1973, 53: 102-108.

Wright, B., *Physical Disability: A Psychological Approach.* (New York: Harper, 1960.)

Zola, K., "The Problems and Prospects of Mutual Aid Groups," *Rehabilitation Psychology,* 1973, 19: 4, 180, 183.

IMPLICATIONS FOR REHABILITATION PRACTICE

This chapter takes the position that the consumer of rehabilitation services should and will assume a growing importance in the planning and implementation of local, state, and national services. Although this development has not been equally attractive to all rehabilitation workers, current trends, including provisions in recent rehabilitation legislation, indicate that client participation in many phases of rehabilitation will be stepped up in the 1970s. Not only is this likely to occur in terms of program planning and evaluation but, also, in the role of clients shaping their personal rehabilitation experience. In time, ombundsman arrangements, client purchase vouchers, and improved counselor training for consumer relations and advocacy may be expected to become a constituent part of the federal-state voluntary agency rehabilitation program.

The implications of this change are already observable in many sections of the country. Increasingly, disabled clients are being perceived as comanagers of their rehabilitation experience and as coplanners of community-wide rehabilitation programs, rather than as targets of an exclusively professionally directed establishment. Thus, any remnants of the older view of the rehabilitation counselor as an omnipotent presence or an untouchable decision-maker will soon be replaced by a collegiality in which clients and counselors form part-

nerships in which both have broad decision-making roles and accountability for the success of the service.

Equally important, as this change occurs, not only will clients'
human rights in the rehabilitation experience be made more explicit
and safeguarded, but a basic long-standing tenet of the rehabilitation
movement will be put into action. As long as formal rehabilitation has
existed, it has maintained the objective of fostering maximum client
independence. In the past, this goal was not always achievable because
a counselor-dominated service process often rendered the client less,
rather than more, independent. In inviting the consumer to join the
rehabilitation team as a respected equal, rehabilitation workers will
find that they have adopted still another powerful service technique for
optimizing client self-direction. In this context, the emergence of the
disabled person as an autonomous and responsible person will begin during, not after, rehabilitation.

CHAPTER VI

ASSESSING VOCATIONAL POTENTIAL

SETTING THE SCENE

The vocational potential of the disabled client has consistently been a major concern of the rehabilitation process in a work-oriented society. Characteristically, disabled individuals in such a society cannot assume expected adult, social roles unless they find an appropriate place in the world of work. In the past the evaluation of vocational potential consisted of noting on a checklist client responses to a variety of vocationally related tasks, activities, and situations. This procedure produced a multitude of detail, some of it seemingly unrelated to work potential, and a rather static picture of client abilities and limitations.

In focusing on a work personality as a vital component in vocational adjustment and potential, Neff adds a dynamic, unifying frame of reference to the still somewhat amorphous perceptions of rehabilitation workers. He implies that in the context of human physical, emotional, and intellectual aptitudes, certain individual behaviors emerge that shape our approach to vocational activities. When these behaviors are incongruent with occupational demands, vocational adjustment and development is impeded and serious job problems arise. To a large extent this incompatibility between work personality and occupational demands accounts for much of the vocational maladjustment observed when evaluating disabled persons who lack the attributes of a "successful" worker.

In reading this chapter, it is well to keep in mind that human behavior has continuity that extends beyond the boundaries of categorized life situations. Personality problems that render an individual ineffective in family, educational, peer, and community relationships are likely to be manifested in the vocational area as well, but if it is found that they don't, then it may be that the work situation is uniquely different and possibly therapeutic. By learning more about the work personality concept, the reader may be better equipped to understand the source of many vocational development problems and how rehabilitation interventions may eliminate or, at least, neutralize such problems.

CHAPTER VI

ASSESSING VOCATIONAL POTENTIAL

Walter S. Neff

One of the striking features of the rehabilitation movement in the United States is its heavy emphasis on work and work adjustment. It is not too much to say that the chief criterion of rehabilitation success involves the entry or restoration of the handicapped person to the world of work. Ours is a heavily work-oriented society in which the attainment of some measure of individual economic independence is a central value. Although there are some countertrends at work, most of us—professionals and clients alike—have internalized this core value and accept its necessity. Inability to accomplish this outcome is regarded by the concerned rehabilitation specialist—and, frequently, by his client—as only a partial success or even a flat failure of the rehabilitation process. This is so much the case that the federal and state agencies concerned with rehabilitation report their successes with the operative phrase, "rehabilitated into employment."

More so, therefore, than others of the helping professions, rehabilitation professionals find themselves deeply enmeshed in what it takes to adapt to work in modern society. What is there about this particular disabling condition, in this particular individual, which constitutes a barrier to gainful employment? What techniques of vocational assessment and what kinds of work training are needed to overcome or ameliorate the barrier in question? What do we need to know about the labor market, about the kinds of work available, so that we can help handicapped persons find their way to a job? Do the attitudes of employers—and work peers—have any influence on placement of the handicapped? What about the orientation to work of the clients themselves, damaged as they may be by the disorganizing and fright-

103

ening consequences of a serious illness or accident, or, perhaps, unable to cope with the demand to work because of a long-term, even congenital, impairment?

Given the fact that the attainment of some kind of adjustment to work is one of the chief aims of the rehabilitation process, what is it that we need to know about it? Here, questions are many and answers surprisingly difficult to come by. Although there is considerable literature on human work, much of it tends to take for granted the very issues which are of major concern to the rehabilitation counselor. The industrial engineer, the industrial psychologist, and the vocational guidance specialist start with the assumption that all (or most) people *can* work. The interests of these specialists are focused on other questions: What kinds of work are different people capable of doing? What factors influence occupational choice? What is the effect of variation in working conditions on productivity and morale? How can we improve work efficiency? What are the effects on work productivity of various patterns of group interaction among workers or of various sets of relationships between workers and their supervisors?

While these are matters of very considerable importance in their own right, the rehabilitation counselors often find themselves faced with what might be called a *prior* set of questions, on which the general literature on human work has tended to be silent. Why are certain people apparently unable to adjust to work under even the best of working conditions? What are the life experiences which facilitate or impede a satisfactory adjustment to work? How do we appraise the ability to work of a person who—by reason of long-term or congenital disability—has never experienced it? What is there about typical work situations which may present barriers to the work adjustment of disabled persons? Is there a set of behaviors and motivations, affects and cognitions, which can be described as the *work personality,* and which can be deficient or distorted in some handicapped individuals? What do we have to do to help the disabled person cope with certain of the special demands and pressures of work in modern society?

In attempting to find useful answers to these complex questions, the field of vocational rehabilitation has been pioneered in three basic directions. First, there have been a number of attempts to improve the techniques of assessment of work potential and to adapt existing methods to the special problems of disabled persons. Second, there have been notable efforts to study the process by which people adapt to work, with a marked emphasis on procedures designed to facilitate an adjustment to work. Third, there have been the beginnings of interest in working out a general theory of work behavior, provoked in part by the finding that people with similar disabilities appear to display quite different dispositions toward an adaptation to work. The remainder of this chapter deals with these interrelated issues.

Techniques of Work Assessment

When rehabilitation specialists began to cast about for techniques of work evaluation, there were initially only two things they could do. First, they could attempt to utilize the very considerable body of occupational tests, which have been worked out for almost every conceivable type of employment during the past generation. Second, they could turn to the very large body of information developed through job analysis, which is summed up in the monumental *Dictionary of Occupational Titles,* produced and supplemented by the U.S. Department of Labor. For a variety of reasons, neither of these sources has proved to be particularly useful in dealing with the vocational problems of disabled persons.

The limitations of the standardized industrial or vocational test are many, if we consider their applicability to vocational rehabilitation. These instruments are essentially large-scale screening devices, with adequate levels of reliability but rather low predictive validities. A major problem for our particular field is that their scores are interpretable only with respect to the normal populations on which these measures were standardized. A basic assumption is that the persons to be tested are representative of the standardization population. Further, as in most testing situations, it is assumed that test subjects are adequately motivated and that there are no unusual barriers to employment. None of these assumptions hold unambiguously for the handicapped. Rehabilitation counselors often find themselves confronted with disabled persons who have had no work experience at all, either because the disability was congenital or of very long duration. Frequently, they also are people who have many doubts concerning their ability to work and many uncertainties concerning the willingness of potential employers to accept them. The utility, therefore, of the typical standardized aptitude test becomes an open question, when we need to assess the work potential of, for example, an ex-mental patient with long-term hospitalization, a borderline retardate with no work history, a person with congenital brain damage, a socially and culturally deprived school dropout, or even a member of a seriously disadvantaged ethnic minority.

What is somewhat more surprising is that the *Dictionary of Occupational Titles* is somewhat less useful in rehabilitation work than its content would imply. The *Dictionary* provides a terminology and classification of thousands of kinds of jobs and includes supplementary volumes detailing the required skills and training for each. However, the bulk of the actual clients seen in rehabilitation agencies are people who have made, at best, a quite marginal work adjustment and tend to represent the lowest rungs of the occupational ladder. Too often, they are people who have never worked at all, or have had very uneven work histories, limited to generally unskilled or slightly skilled employment. Much of the immense and useful information contained in the *Dictionary* is, therefore, not immediately applicable to the work problems of many disabled clients.

Faced with these difficulties, the rehabilitation movement has tended to experiment with its own systems of work assessment. Here we find two approaches. The first is the *work sample* approach, designed to provide the evaluator with some idea of the client's potential for training for one or another type of occupation. The second involves an effort to assess the client's ability to adapt to the *general* conditions of work and, for want of a better term, we shall call it the technique of *situational assessment.* We shall briefly examine what is at stake in each approach.

The Work Sample. The basic notion here is that the best method of finding out whether persons can do something is to put them to work doing it and observe their performance. The work sample differs from the standard aptitude test in that the former are close simulations ("mock-ups") of the actual task of interest. Unlike the aptitude test, which operates at a fairly high level of abstraction and tends to focus on a single component ability or trait, the work sample comprises an effort to duplicate the actual materials and procedures found in a given kind of work and is thus a good deal closer to the actual realities to be confronted on the job.

During the past two decades there have been a number of efforts to

develop work sample systems that are suited to the study of handicapped clients. Perhaps the best known is the TOWER system, worked
out by the Institute for the Crippled and Disabled of New York City. A
useful library of various sets of job samples has been prepared by
Robert Overs of the Vocational Guidance and Rehabilitation Service
of Cleveland. More recently, the Jewish Employment and Vocational
Service of Philadelphia has pioneered in the development of a set of
work samples designed to assess the work potential of the entirely
unskilled person. The objective of most of these systems is to find a
suitable area of vocational training, which will equip the client to enter
an occupation in which he has had no prior experience.

While the work sample possesses the signal advantage of being closer
to the realities of work than the typical industrial test, this is not to say
that there are no disadvantages. First, there is the danger of rapid
obsolescence. Technological change in industry is very rapid and there
is the constant risk of developing an adequate appraisal technique for
jobs that no longer exist. Second, there are apparently some very
difficult problems of validation. It appears to be easier to predict how
well a client will do in a recommended training program than on an
actual job after training. This is because, as we shall discuss below,
work involves much more than the application of a particular work
skill, no matter how well mastered.

Despite these difficulties, the work sample methods have much to
recommend them and are being increasingly widely used. Their virtues
are their strong reality orientation, their focus on the simulation of
actual work requirements, their reliance on global behavior as opposed
to the abstraction of isolated component traits, and the opportunity to
observe work behavior in a reasonably controlled environment.
Further elaboration of these methods should serve to reduce some of
their present limitations.

Situational Assessment. This technique asks a more elementary set of
questions than does the work sample approach. Can potential workers
really work at all? What is there in all work situations that comprises a
particular problem for them? How do they react to people on the job
(supervisors and coworkers)? Can they work only under unrealistically
benign conditions? The objectives of situational assessment are to
obtain information on what might be called the general work personality (see below): the meaning of work to individuals, the manner in

which they react to the *social* conditions met on the job, and the work roles they find it congenial or difficult to play.

Situational assessment came into being as a kind of systematized observation of the behavior of handicapped clients in the sheltered or rehabilitation workshop, which generally attempts to simulate very closely the general conditions of work found in actual competitive industry. What is required is that all of the customary conditions of work are present on the scene, with the possibility available of planned variation in these conditions to observe client response. In situational assessment, the primary instrument of evaluation is the trained observer—typically, a trained rehabilitation expert who serves as foreman in the rehabilitation workshop. The typical outcome is not a "score" but an "appraisal." Clients may be found, for example, to react inappropriately to supervision or their primary difficultiies may be discovered to lie in an inability to tolerate pressure for output. The basic objective is to see how well clients fit the general role of worker and to estimate what needs to be done to help them toward a better fit.

Like the work sample approach, situational assessment is not without its own peculiar problems. It is not easy to reproduce, within the confines of the typical rehabilitation facility, the very wide variety of kinds of work and the various levels of skill requirements found in industry at large. The situational assessor is looking for the common denominators of any kind of work and these are not always easy to come by. Most rehabilitation workshops feature very elemental kinds of work—unskilled assembly, packaging, simple clerical, and so forth. This seems to have worked reasonably well in practice, largely because, as we have observed, the typical rehabilitation center tends to serve rather marginal populations: the mentally retarded, the severely undereducated and underprivileged, and the like. But we are not certain the situational assessment—as it now functions—would serve the needs of those clients whose ability to work effectively depends heavily on the kinds of work they can expect to perform.

Techniques of Work Adjustment

One of the most interesting developments of recent years has been something of a major shift in the objectives and aims of the rehabilitation counselor. Until a decade or two ago, the tacit assumption prevailed that the rehabilitation expert could function usefully only with clients who already manifested adequate motivation for employment. As the professional task was then conceived, the objective was to prepare clients for some new kind of work which their handicap would permit them to perform. In practice, however, it gradually became evident that this approach tended to restrict the provision of rehabilitation services to a rather small fraction of the target population. This problem became intensified as the rehabilitation movement began to take on clients with extremely inadequate work histories, either because their disabilities had been incurred at infancy or in early childhood, or because clients had been sealed off from the world of work by such syndromes as mental retardation, emotional disorder, or extreme social deprivation.

The result of these experiences is that the field of rehabilitation gradually became aware that the problems of work adjustment are not limited to the realms of cognitive and motor skills but also reflect certain aspects of general emotional behavior: feelings, emotions, perceptions and misperceptions of the self, and interpersonal relations. These are terms which are familiar to the personality theorist but which were, for a considerable period, relatively alien to the rehabilitation specialist of the past period.

The gradual realization that work adjustment may require more than the provision of particular technical skills has produced an active search for methods of *treatment*—methods that have the aim of motivating the unmotivated. As I have defined this search, it is for the means to diminish or overcome what I regard as the *psychosocial barriers* to an adequate work adjustment. We have become increasingly aware that work in modern society is a complex social and interpersonal situation, which has its own unique set of demand characteristics, as well as a unique array of pressures and rewards. How are we to deal with the person who may be technically capable of performing some work task, but who is too fearful or angry, too naive or indifferent to meet the customary demands of the typical work situation? In the field of rehabilitation, efforts to treat these problems have taken two directions. The first may be described as therapeutic counseling and has its strongest kinship to the procedures of conventional psychotherapy. The second is basically a nonverbal procedure and finds its closest analogue in what is coming to be known as *milieu therapy*.

In the field of rehabilitation, the chief modality of milieu therapy is provided by the rehabilitative workshop. A considerable literature has accumulated on this innovative device, but we can deal with it only very briefly here. Fundamentally, the rehabilitative workshop is an arena in which to observe basic work behavior and is also a medium in which desired changes in work behavior can be brought about. To function as a therapeutic medium, certain conditions must be carefully provided. Above all, the facility must be as realistic a simulation of actual working conditions as ingenuity can contrive. Wages should be paid, although the amounts may be graded in terms of some rational plan. The work performed should be manifestly realistic in the sense that it is not "make-work" but results in actual commodities destined for sale. The client should be made aware that, in the long run at least, he is expected to reach customary standards of output and quality. Both coworkers and supervisors are present on the scene, so that the client is confronted with the full range of interpersonal relations he will encounter on the job. Working hours and work rules should approximate those prevailing in ordinary employment.

Of course, if it is to be therapeutic, the rehabilitative workshop must include certain features not found in ordinary industry. The chief difference may be found in the roles and functions of the work supervisor—the shop foreman. Although to maintain the verisimilitude of the situation, the shop foreman must be seen by the client as an ordinary work supervisor in an ordinary work situation, the workshop foreman in the rehabilitative workshop has a complex set of professional tasks to carry out. He must have the training and time to observe the client intensively so that he can detect what is preventing an adjustment to work. He then must be in a position to manipulate those conditions of work so that the client will move toward more adequate work behaviors.

Essentially, what we have here is a situation in which the client can test the reality of what it means to work through being confronted with a variety of variable work procedures. Compensation can be varied; the client can be placed to work by himself or with others; the foreman can adopt, by plan, a range of supervisory postures, ranging from a high degree of supportive permissiveness to an equally high degree of authoritative control; work rules can be enforced with different degrees of rigidity; standards for quality and quantity can be systematically varied. The rehabilitative workshop, if it is to be effective, operates flexibly between two extremes. On the one hand, it does not summarily discharge the client if he cannot, fairly quickly, meet customary working standards. On the other hand, there is no intention to provide permanent sheltered employment. The rehabilitative workshop is clearly seen as a transitional facility—transitional to unprotected employment—and if the client cannot, in a reasonable period, approach or reach customary working standards, some other disposition of the case must be undertaken.

It should be noted that, in contrast to the work sample approach, or to vocational training generally, the rehabilitative workshop is not in the business of teaching specific work skills. If anything is learned by the client, it is something more general and certainly more basic: the social requirements of being able to work at all.

A Theory of Work Behavior

Work is so pervasive and central a human phenomenon that a very large body of writing has grown concerning it. Theologians and philosophers have seen work as a major feature of the human condition. For political scientists and economists, work is a core issue for social analysis. Sociologists and psychologists have become sufficiently interested in the problems of work so that new subspecialties have developed: the sociology of work and industrial psychology. Elsewhere (Neff, 1968), I have commented at length on some of these viewpoints concerning work, although we cannot do more here than note their existence.

For the rehabilitation expert, however, it soon becomes clear that work, in highly complex societies such as our own, is perhaps best understood as a form of social behavior. Much more is required of the individual than the ability to deliver a particular kind of work skill. There are really two sides to the process of adaptation to work. On the one hand, we work in quite complicated social situations, in which the individual must be able to cope with a unique set of social demands. We shall call these the *demand characteristics of work situations*. On the other hand, we must bring to these settings not only the know-how required by a specific work task, but also an elaborate set of attitudes, opinions, beliefs, and affects which we shall call the *work personality*. What is needed for a successful adaptation to work is an appropriate interaction between these two sets of factors.

In analyzing the demand characteristics of work environments, one can distinguish the structural features of the environment from its interpersonal aspects, and both from a set of customs and rituals that characterize work as a kind of subculture. A successful adaptation to work requires at least a minimum amount of ability to cope with these external demands.

Under structural aspects, there are at least four important features of most work settings that can present major problems for the handicapped person. First, there is the *necessity for travel.* Most kinds of contemporary work are sited away from the home and require the use of public or private transportation. For many varieties of physical disability, for the more severely mentally retarded, and for some of the emotionally and mentally disturbed, this requirement can be heavy and needs special instruction and, often, special arrangements. Second, there is the problem that most work is *public,* that it is carried on under conditions where the worker must expect to be under the almost continuous observation of supervisors, coworkers, and the general public. Third, the typical work situation is not only public, it is relatively *impersonal.* The human beings who people most work settings tend to be aggregates of relative strangers, with whom close intimacy is both discouraged and tends to be inappropriate. This impersonality may place heavy burdens on those who have strong needs for more intimate relations: the immature, the dependent, or even the more severely troubled. The final structural aspect of most kinds of work is the degree to which they are bound by *time.* The strongly time-bound character of most jobs sets them off rather sharply from the environments of home or play.

The interpersonal features of work settings are at least as important as their structural features. Here we deal with only two issues: the *demands of supervision* and *relations to work peers.* The former operates, as it were, between two boundaries. On the one hand, after an initial period of close supervision, the worker is expected to be more or less self-regulating. On the other hand, the degree to which he can really work on his own has fixed limits, which vary from job to job. The client who is rendered so fearful or so angry by ordinary supervision that he cannot work effectively is obviously destined for early discharge. Similarly, the ability to get on with one's work peers is an indispensable requirement for adaptation to work. The immature or disturbed person may demand more from his fellows than they can reasonably give, or he may find them more indifferent to his personal problems than he can tolerate.

Finally, like any other sector of society, the work situation displays specific customs, rules, and traditions. Many kinds of work are marked by special lingos and prescribed forms of dress and appearance. It is probably not too much to say that many people leave their jobs or are fired, as often because they cannot behave toward their colleagues in expected ways, as because they lack the requisite work skills. Adaptation to work is as much a process of enculturation as that required of an immigrant who comes to a new country.

We have said that coping with work demands is one side of the process of adaptation to work. But we have also said that work adaptation is a two-sided transaction. What must the prospective worker bring with him to the work situation? Here we enter the domain of the *work personality*. We will maintain here that, like many other forms of complex social behavior, the ability to adapt to work is not simply built into the genes but is arrived at through a long process of social learning. In effect, we *learn* to become workers and, as is true for other forms of human learning, there is ample opportunity for things to go wrong. Many disabled persons, whose handicaps are congenital or very long in duration, may never have internalized those response patterns which are conducive to an easy work adjustment.

One of the more important things about the work personality is that it appears to have a semiautonomous character. By this we mean that its chief features, as well as the conditions which determine its development, are not identical with those that characterize other areas of the personality—those concerned with personal intimacy, for example—nor does it follow that disturbances in one personality area necessarily entail disturbances in all others. Some frank psychotics, for example, are able to meet work demands with reasonable adequacy, while remaining quite unable to manage other human relations. It seems likely that the components of the work personality are laid down during a later period of child development than are other personality areas and constitute responses to a different set of constraints and pressures. The experiences of infancy and early childhood may indeed be critical for personality generally, but they do not appear to be the *sufficient* conditions of the work personality. The latter are apparently associated with the experiences of middle childhood and adolescence, particularly during that phase of child development that Freud called the "latency period."

In order to grasp this point, we have to know what happens when children of five or six are required to leave their families for hours at a time to go to school. A great deal more is learned (or *not* learned) in school than a specific set of cognitive skills. It would seem that many of the requirements of the work role are first encountered in the school environment. Children get their first serious conditioning to the clock; they must learn to accommodate themselves to all kinds of strangers (their teachers and schoolmates); they must begin to adapt to those aspects of life that are public and impersonal, casual and distant. The child's schooling begins the long process of erosion of family ties and that end in a more or less independent existence as a working adult.

Beyond these more subtle conditions, there is one basic demand of the school that is central to all else: the *demand to achieve*. It is in the school setting that the distinctions between work and play, between work and love first begin to take shape in the mind of the child. Preschool children may play at adult work, but everyone is aware that they are playing and, while they may be encouraged in it, no one demands that they continue. On the other hand, school children are quickly made aware that mastering the alphabet or learning the multiplication table is a serious business and they are expected to produce. Thus, certain basic requirements of the work role are laid down in the early school years: The ability to concentrate on a task for fixed periods of time, the development of response patterns to supervisory authority, the limits of cooperation and competition with peers, the meanings and values associated with achievement, the rewards and sanctions for performance, and the affects (both positive and negative) associated with being productive. Of course, the school does not operate in a social vacuum but is itself part of society and reflects it.

According to this view, the work personality comes into being in response to the precepts of society that the individual must play some kind of productive role. In its earliest form, the child is confronted with this demand when he or she enters some type of educative process. The compulsion to work is initially external but is internalized to varying degrees and in different forms. Once this demand is internalized in some form or other, it can arouse its own feelings of pleasure,, gratification, anxiety, guilt, or inadequacy. As a consequence, coping behaviors and defenses are mobilized and eventually consolidate into the particular work style of the individual person.

The implications of this theory of work behavior are many. First, it is argued that maladaptation to work may reflect some inability to cope with one or another of the demand characteristics of work as a *social* situation. Second, it is implied that the problems of work need not respond to the same therapeutic techniques that have been developed to solve the problems of intimate personal relations, since they may arise in different areas of the personality and constitute responses to events of a different order. Third, we infer that the presence or absence of a given work skill is by no means a sufficient condition of the ability to work, but that adaptation to work requires a quite complex set of attitudes, interpersonal skill, and assigned meanings. Finally, it follows that vocational rehabilitation may require much more than a vocational training or retraining process oriented toward the acquisition of a particular skill, but may have to attend to much more basic questions related to the ability of the person to work at all.

IMPLICATIONS FOR REHABILITATION PRACTICE

(1) The common assumption that all (or even most) people are able to work in a satisfactory manner should be reexamined in the light of practical experience to the contrary.

(2) This assumption may be tested by studying the process through which people adapt to work in an effort to determine if common, work-related characteristics are identifiable among vocational "non-adapters."

(3) Because of the limitations of standard tests when applied to disabled populations, work sample, workshop, learning capacities, and other special techniques are required to assess individual vocational personality and potential.

(4) Preliminary to assessing and strengthening specific job skills or goals, a rehabilitation evaluation should determine the nature of the individual's work personality and the degree to which this personality meets general work requirements.

(5) In this context adaptation to work may be viewed as an interac-

tion between the social and vocational demands of employment and the relevant attitudes, opinions, beliefs, and affects that make up an individual's work personality. For example, work usually demands the ability to travel to and from a place of employment, accept continuing supervisory observation, relate appropriately to coworkers or the public, tolerate the businesslike nature of vocational relationships, and perform the job in accordance with set time limits. In this regard, it has been found that more jobs are lost because disabled (as well as other) people cannot behave as required while at work than because of skill or ability deficits.

(6) A work personality is developed as part of the total socialization process. For example, school experiences provide much more than cognitive skills. During the school years one learns how to work and achieve, acquiring in the process basic aspects of a work personality. Thus the child learns that society expects him/her to play a productive role, and that in adult years this role finds expression in work activities.

As suggested in this chapter, there are many implications of a work personality approach for vocational rehabilitation. Instead of emphasizing work skill, as is so often the case in evaluation, counselors might more properly focus on work personality and more general readiness for occupational involvement. Concurrently, more attention should be paid to a disabled student's school behavior in terms of future vocational development, rather than on the narrower variables of educational achievement. Most important of all, perhaps, is the conclusion that work personality, as a function of total personality, is a concept that necessitates a broadening of vocational rehabilitation itself. Narrowly conceived, vocational activities may have limited value unless incorporated into broader personality interventions which help to reshape fundamental client responses that often determine vocational success or failure.

CHAPTER VII

REHABILITATING THE SOCIALLY DISABLED

SETTING THE SCENE

From its earliest beginnings, the vocational rehabilitation movement has maintained a series of middle-class assumptions. These assumptions include a belief that most disabled persons are highly motivated to enter employment, that delay of personal satisfaction during preparation for a vocation is tolerable for all, and that participation in a process that requires months, even years, of cooperative counselor-client effort is within everyone's capabilities. As long as rehabilitation service applicants were drawn primarily from middle-class areas, these assumptions had great validity. Thus, from 1920 to the end of the 1950s, middle-class values and assumptions fueled the vocational rehabilitation process for a largely middle-class caseload. Occasionally, other clients applied for service, but with few exceptions, they found the rehabilitation service to be less compatible with their lifestyles.

In the early 1960s, the United States rediscovered the poor and the socially atypical and undertook a massive effort to target human services more directly to this group. In time, both public and voluntary rehabilitation agencies were caught up in this enterprise and began to redesign their service structures and delivery systems to make them more responsive to the "new" client, For the first time, some rehabilitation agencies became interested in the narcotics addict, the alcoholic, the minority group member, the economically and socially deprived, the legal offender, and the social dropout.

Naiveté coupled with an excessive commitment to the "old" ways of doing things led many rehabilitation workers to believe that only minor modifications in existing practices and procedures were required to extend well-established rehabilitation services to most socially disadvantaged individuals. Subsequent failures and disappointments soon underscored the futility of this approach. The chapter that follows provides a background for understanding why a "Band-Aid" approach was doomed in the

119

rehabilitation of the socially disadvantaged from the start and suggests directions in which vocational rehabilitation is, and should be, moving in order to maximize its contributions to this special client group. Alternate rehabilitation service designs are reviewed so that the reader can judge for himself how far vocational rehabilitation has come in serving this client group.

CHAPTER VII

REHABILITATING THE SOCIALLY DISABLED

David Malikin

Once upon a time people lived the "American Dream," its message was that if you worked hard and honestly you would be rewarded with success. That dream became a nightmare during the depression of the 1930s and was completely shattered for many during the 1960s. By then large numbers had discovered that American society was changing at a pace that was leaving them far behind. They found themselves unable to cope with a complex, competitive system, feeling like outcasts, in a state of limbo. They were small farmers who had been pushed off their land, workers whose factories and plants had closed down or moved elsewhere, older people who had retired on pensions that soon left them living in a state of "genteel poverty," young people who hated a war they couldn't understand and for whom the future seemed bleak and without promise, and members of minority groups who had long been poor and had given up hope that things would ever get better. While different from one another in many ways, their common bond was a sense of helplessness and anomie that beset them as they viewed the larger society about them. They were socially disabled.

Two major forces contribute to the condition of social disability, one external, the other internal. The external force is generated by a society that promises one set of values and then practices another; that preaches equality, freedom, opportunity, and concern for the underprivileged, but then fosters rugged individualism, getting ahead by any means, and leaves many feeling less equal, less free, and sometimes less human. The internal force is generated by the socially disabled themselves. Lacking motivation and resources necessary for successful cop-

121

ing mechanisms, they develop lifestyles that are shaped by the need to survive at any cost. Sometimes this means using alcohol or drugs to ease the anxiety and pain of their existence, and sometimes it might lead to crime to obtain material goods denied to them by minimal incomes. It is a situation fraught with protest and conflict, one that can only be resolved by dealing with both the internal and external forces.

Lest generalization lead to stereotype it should be noted that not all alcoholics, addicts, public offenders, or poor people are socially disabled. It is estimated that 10 or 15 million Americans of all classes are alcoholics,[1] but only a minority of them create problems for society. Many are not even identified, because they are able to support their habit and delimit its damaging effects. This observation applies to drug addicts as well. Barbara Kerr [2] studied a group of middle-class, female addicts and contrasted their experiences with those of lower-class, female addicts. She reported the biggest difference she had found was that it was much easier for middle-class addicts to get off drugs. Because they possessed middle-class incomes, were the right color, and had mobility, they could pick up and move on to something else when they found that drugs were not the answer to their problems. They could also seek help from psychiatrists or go to sanitariums and were not dependent on public programs as were lower-class individuals.

Crime too has its fair share of "respectable citizens" whose offenses are regarded very differently from those committed by working class offenders. Because white-collar crime is not violent and does not threaten the average citizen, who is often even unaware of the effect of such activity, it is regarded much more leniently. Actually, offenses of corruption, graft, and illegal practices among government officials and business executives appear on the rise, as noted in a recent issue of the *New Times* magazine [3] which listed 200 such individuals currently indicted or convicted for criminal acts. These individuals have little or no difficulty reentering the mainstream of American economic life after serving sentences, as do lower-class offenders.

Even poverty should not be fully equated with social disadvantage. Oscar Lewis [4] identified 50 traits that characterize the culture of poverty, with low economic status being only one of them. As an example he cited the case of recently arrived immigrants who reside in slums for periods of time, but then move on to improved conditions as they become integrated into the economic system. Their experience is significantly different from those who suffer from generational poverty. In summary, then, the socially disabled are those alcoholics, addicts, public offenders, or disadvantaged individuals (sometimes the same person), who for a variety of important reasons are unable to mobilize themselves for independent solutions of their problems and who cannot attain upward mobility with their own resources. These are the individuals who become the focus of rehabilitation programs targeted to assist the socially disadvantaged.

It is essential to briefly view some of the handicapping conditions that affect the lives of the socially disabled and which make their rehabilitation the difficult task it is. To begin with, in addition to subsisting on minimal incomes, many suffer from malnutrition and even slow starvation. A medical team that toured the Mississippi Delta in 1967 [5] reported to a Senate subcommittee that it found large numbers of children who were hungry, in pain, sick, and slowly starving to death. One of the most severe and permanent consequences of malnutrition, specifically the lack of protein, is the brain damage that occurs in children before they reach the age of four. These researchers expressed the opinion that not only did this affect educational performance, but it was a major factor in perpetuating generational poverty. The results of a Head Start programmatic research [6] indicated that malnutrition is a national problem, with from 20 percent to 40 percent of the children studied found to be anemic. In his classic study, *The Other America: Poverty in the United States,*[7] Harrington described the effect of ill health on the vicious cycle of poverty as follows:

> The poor get sick more than anyone else in the society. That is because they live in slums, jammed together under unhygienic conditions; they have inadequate diets and cannot get decent medical care. When they become sick, they are sick longer than any other group in the society. Because they are sick more often and longer than anyone else, they lose wages and work, and find it difficult to hold a steady job. And because of this they cannot pay for good housing, for a nutritious diet, for doctors. At any given point in the cycle, particularly when there is a major illness, their prospect is to move to an even lower level and to begin the cycle round and round, toward even more suffering.

Another aspect of social disability is its disruptive effect on family life. With a large number of poor families lacking a father in the home and mothers attempting to earn a living, child care is often haphazard at best, with surrogate parents more the rule than the exception. Children grow up in an environment that is frequently lacking in parental guidance, affection, and stimulation. As a consequence, Rainwater [8] cautioned, social workers and other professionals should avoid the tendency to use the norms of "American family life" as a means of comparing people who simply cannot conform to such norms, even if they desired to. The result of this chaotic situation, she concluded, is the development of a negative view of human nature generally, and of a negative self-image specifically. She agreed with Harrington and others that one of the main components of poverty is a maiming of personality.

Kunce and Cope [9] noted that though there doesn't appear to be a personality of poverty, some common psychological attributes associated with the role of disadvantagement stand out: a different (implied deficient) performance on educational, psychological, and other behavioral tasks; a different language which adds to the difficulties in communicating and learning in a middle-class environment; pervasive negative and self-defeating attitudes toward achievement; and higher incidences of maladaptive behaviors such as passivity, crime, and emotional disturbance. The authors also found that, because so many needs of the poor are unmet and the future seems so distant and hopeless, their ability to work for long-term goals is diminished, and they prefer tangible, short-term ones which are more easily satisfied.

Recognizing the need for short-term solutions, the government and some social agencies regard obtaining jobs as the most effective way of dealing with the problems of poverty. This simplistic approach reflects the ignorance of many observers about the devastating effects of poverty. If there is a lack of awareness of the handicaps of disadvantagement, then there is a parallel lack in the comprehension of the complexity of these handicaps and of the difficulty in overcoming them. Further, in a work-oriented society, it has long been assumed that every adult has the capability of functioning adequately on a job. Neff, in *Work and Human Behavior,*[10] theorized that part of, yet separate from, an individual's personality is a set of attitudes and behaviors that constitute his work personality. He proposed that the formation of this work personality is part of a developmental process that includes childhood experiences, such as attending school, assuming certain responsibilities in the home as one matures, joining peers in a variety of activities, obtaining part-time, after school jobs, and so forth.

Those persons lacking in such developmental experiences appear to possess a "weak" work personality and are often unable to adequately fulfill a vocational role. This inadequacy might be revealed in the lack of attitudes and aptitudes necessary for successful job performance, in the inability to relate to supervisors or fellow workers, in the inability to tolerate the frustrations inherent in most work routines, and in numerous other ways. It would appear that before many socially disabled individuals can obtain and hold jobs with any degree of consistency, they have to be assisted in strengthening their work personalities. As awareness for this type of assistance has grown, the field of vocational rehabilitation (governmental and voluntary agencies) has gradually assumed greater responsibility in this task, and simultaneously, rehabilitation counselors have had to cope with large, new populations that differed importantly from the physically and emotionally disabled.

One of the major differences encountered by counselors working with the socially disabled is that of their attitude toward counseling. Since most handicapped individuals who apply for vocational rehabilitation services do so with an expectation of being helped, it is usually assumed that the socially disabled have a similar favorable regard for counseling and other services being offered. Gross,[11] who studied Youth Opportunity Centers across the United States, found this to be a fallacy based on a set of false assumptions. These assumptions are:

(1) The assumption that disadvantaged clients come for counseling of their own accord. Actually, large numbers are sent by parole or police officers, by welfare personnel, and others under threat of losing some benefit, payment, or their freedom.

(2) The assumption that the client wants help. On the contrary, some are hostile and resistive; others are passive and unmotivated.

(3) The assumption that the client accepts the authority of the counselor. The counselor is not seen as a professional who wants to help but rather as a bureaucratic official whose authority is part of the police power.

(4) The assumption that clients come as individuals to be treated individually. Many regard themselves as spokesmen or representatives of others who are fighting the "establishment."

Consequently, the counselor and counseling service are frequently perceived as the enemy.

(5) The assumption that counselors accept their clients. Though the attempt may be made, many counselors fail to accept the disadvantaged, finding their attitudes and behavior objectionable.

Vontress [12] described the white middle-class counselor as coming from another world, one who is seen by young ghetto blacks as a product of an American culture shot through with pernicious racism. Lower-class blacks have been deceived so often by whites that the counselor role of much talk and little action seems like just another "con" game to be treated suspiciously and cautiously. In general, socially disabled clients appear to reject a verbal, problem-solving, counseling approach. Overwhelmed by the struggles of survival, they shrug aside "empty" words and seek actions that might produce favorable and alleviating changes in their everyday lives. To empathize with a needy client, even to shed tears with him, does not relieve the pain of hunger, of being without a job, or of a decent place to live. It does not even communicate a real sense of concern unless one of the results of the counseling relationship is some tangible assistance. For many, there is a need to experience some constructive gain as a form of preconditioning before verbalization can become an effective tool. Too often, programs for the socially disabled subject clients to lengthy periods of intake, interview, and evaluation procedures while urgent life problems remain unattended to. Perhaps we should reverse our priorities and offer immediate, practical assistance and then introduce the no less important counseling, planning, and training features.

Noting that many socially disadvantaged individuals were largely unable to take full advantage of emerging training and employment opportunities, Adkins [13] developed a new "life coping skills" approach based on the following principles:

(1) It should be life problem-centered and adaptable to the problems related to living and working in the city.

(2) It should build on knowledge and skills already possessed and provide ways of improving problem-solving skills.

(3) It should take advantage of their good peer relations by maxi-

mizing group activities in areas of common concern, while at
the same time providing attention to personal needs through
individual counseling when needed.

In addition to group and individual counseling, Adkins suggests
using films, video tapes, records, field visits, and role modeling as a way
of focusing on genuine life problems and offering the clients a variety of
ways of coping with these problems. This approach is pragmatic,
understandable, and realistic in that specific programs are prepared for
particular groups and are based on the life experiences of each group.
Programs with addicts, the socially disadvantaged, and with learning
disabled individuals are currently in operation with encouraging results indicated.

A major difficulty in many vocational rehabilitation programs is
that clients have no assurance of jobs even after they have completed
all preparatory steps. Thus many socially disabled clients, whose
negative past experiences have conditioned them to be pessimistic,
cannot relate realistically to evaluation and training procedures because they do not believe anything tangible will result from them.
When involved in job-seeking activities, they quickly become frustrated and are then accused of lacking motivation. In an effort to overcome this problem, the Federation Employment and Guidance Service
of New York created an experimental "instant placement" program
for a group of drug addicts. Following a short period of detoxification
and social stability the addicts were immediately placed in specially
selected jobs provided by cooperating institutions and employers.
While on these jobs, earning money and meeting needs, the clients
were counseled about careers, personal problems, pending court cases,
and any other matters they raised. At the end of their period of employment some were hired permanently, some went off to school for
further education, some entered vocational training, and some worked
with placement counselors to seek other, suitable jobs for themselves.
The program proved highly effective in that almost all the addicts remained free of drugs, pursued goals they had selected for themselves,
and completed their programs. It was found that the "instant placement" technique was instrumental in showing the clients that they
could be productive individuals. The counseling in this context was
accepted as realistic and helpful in maintaining motivation and coping
with problems. Many clients expressed the feeling that for the first time

in their lives they felt they had some direction and knew what they wanted to accomplish. Lest the idea of guaranteed jobs after rehabilitation be regarded as idealistically unrealistic, it is well to note that this practice has existed for years in a number of European countries.

The new careers concept of Frank Reissman [14] was an important innovative approach to rehabilitating the socially disabled. It was based on several needs, the need to involve them in the solution of their problems, the need for quick employment that their lack of formal education often prevented, and the need to help them perceive life more hopefully. Examining the large number of health, welfare, and educational programs that had sprung up in the 1960s, Reissman and his coworkers found many opportunities for the utilization of clients with potential in a variety of paraprofessional roles. With government support thousands of such jobs were filled and a new labor market created for the socially disabled. Clients formerly on welfare and considered helplessly inept now became involved in the rehabilitation of others, serving as aides, coordinators, messengers, and office assistants, revealing much ability despite the lack of educational skills. The impetus provided by this new labor market led to the formation of new educational programs to train paraprofessionals and created a career ladder that some climbed to achieve professional status. Another major effect of the new careers example was to demonstrate to clients and society at large that the socially disabled could be effectively rehabilitated, and this in turn led to the opening of still more educational and vocational opportunities.

In urging that new ways of working with the socially disabled be explored, the conclusion should not be drawn that traditional rehabilitation practices with one-to-one counseling be discarded. The point, rather, is that the socially disabled are comparable to other disability groups in that they too have individual needs, capacities, limitations, and life circumstances. We can no more be dogmatic or rigid with them than with any other disability group and should adopt whatever rehabilitation approach seems most efficacious even if this occasionally violates one's notions of tradition or professionalism. The socially disabled, as well as all other human beings, require that they be treated with dignity and respect. The lesson for them, and all of us, is that counseling and rehabilitation will continue to be useful modalities so long as they are part of a comprehensive, community-wide approach, involving industry, labor, and governmental forces, working together to make this a more viable society for all.

NOTES

1. Selden D. Bacon. "The Problems of Alcoholism in American Society," in David Malikin. *Social Disability,* New York: New York University Press, 1973, pg. 26.
2. Judy Klemesrud. "A Hard Look at Drugs and the Middle-Class Woman," *New York Times,* August 26, 1974, p. 34.
3. Compiled by Ernest Lendler. "A Catalogue of Corruption," *New Times Magazine,* September 6, 1974, pp. 21-23.
4. Oscar Lewis. "The Culture of Poverty," in Marc Pilisuk and Phyllis Pilisuk, *Poor Americans: How the White Poor Live,* New York: Transaction Books, N.Y. Aldine, 1971, pp. 21-28.
5. William Hedgepeth. "Poverty-Christmas 1967," *Look,* December 26, 1967, pp. 40-44.
6. Henry E. Sigerist. "Malnutrition in American Children," in Herbert Birch and Joan Dye Gussow, eds., *Disadvantaged Children,* New York: Grune and Stratton, 1970, pp. 221-234.
7. Michael Harrington. *The Other America: Poverty in the United States,* Baltimore: Penguin, 1962, p. 22.
8. Lee Rainwater. "Crucible of Identity: The Negro Lower-Class Family," in N. Glazer and C. Creedon, *Children and Poverty: Some Sociological and Psychological Perspectives,* Chicago: Rand-McNally, 1969, pp. 244-270.
9. Joseph T. Kunce and Corrine S. Cope. *Rehabilitation and the Culturally Disadvantaged,* University of Missouri, Rehabilitation Research Institute, Series No. 1, September, 1969.
10. Walter S. Neff. *Work and Human Behavior.* New York: Atherton Press, 1968.
11. Edward Gross. "Report on Problems of Counseling Special Populations," paper presented to Panel on Counseling and Selection of the National Manpower Advisory Committee, Washington, D.C. Spring, 1967.
12. Clemmont Vontress. "Counseling the Culturally Different in Our Society," *Journal of Employment Counseling,* March, 1969 p. 11.
13. Winthrop R. Adkins. "Life Skills: Structured Counseling for the Disadvantaged," *Personnel and Guidance Journal,* Vol. 49, no. 2, October, 1970, pp. 108-116.
14. Frank Reissman and Arthur Pearl. *New Careers for the Poor,* New York: The Free Press, 1965.

IMPLICATIONS FOR REHABILITATION PRACTICE

The socially disadvantaged are a heterogeneous group, the members of which share a common position on the periphery of middle-class society. The disadvantages that eventuate from their basic disabilities and their concomitant low social status precipitate such acute adjustment problems for them that day-to-day survival becomes a central focus of their lives. In the course of coping with the numerous threats to their survival, the socially disadvantaged often develop lifestyles that are incompatible with the demands of a vocational rehabilitation process. For example, sustained postponement of satisfaction for the purpose of long-range vocational benefits often is difficult for them to accept, suggesting that prolonged periods of evaluation, training, and restoration may impose unwarranted stress upon their relationships with rehabilitation agencies.

Consequently, modified rehabilitation procedures and techniques often are required to insure the proper delivery of vocational rehabilitation services to such individuals. In keeping with the social isolation, experience deprivation, and "nonconformist" account in planning vocational rehabilitation services for them:

(1) Centralized rehabilitation offices that are geographically and psychologically remote from the socially disadvantaged person should be replaced by neighborhood or other locally based facilities that are more physically accessible and socially acceptable to the disabled person. If at all possible, these decentralized offices should be integrated into the local community, facilitating case-finding, wider client participation, and more comprehensive follow-up.

(2) Rather than wait for socially disadvantaged individuals to take initiative in making applications for service, rehabilitation agencies should reach out to them. Passivity in case-finding activities tends to bring disproportionately small numbers of socially disadvantaged individuals into a rehabilitation program.

(3) Depending upon individual need, some basic vocational rehabilitation services should be modified in working with socially
disadvantaged clients. For example, counseling that depends
largely upon verbal interchanges may have to be supplanted by
"activity" counseling, especially when clients do not readily
communicate with the counselor through the medium of words
in face-to-face interviews.

(4) Some rehabilitation programs attempt to "remake" the client
in line with the middle-class remunerative worker model. In
doing this, rehabilitation personnel should consider the possibility that this connotes a lack of respect and concern for the
client's own lifestyle. Any "missionary" effort can be perceived
by the targeted individual as a denigration of his current status
and beliefs.

(5) Placing a disabled person in a "socially disadvantaged" rubric
does not lessen the unalterable fact of his individuality. Thus,
each socially disadvantaged client should be carefully evaluated in individual terms and served by a program that is
custom-designed for him.

As in the case of almost all rehabilitation caseloads, the socially
disadvantaged are far more comparable to other disabled groups than
they are different. In fact, as one reviews the suggestions made for
serving them, it becomes clear that sound rehabilitation casework is as
applicable to them as to the more traditional client groups and that the
modifications that are required are just extensions of sound rehabilitation practice rather than radical changes in the service structure.

CHAPTER VIII

REHABILITATION OF PERSONS WITH SERIOUS
EMOTIONAL DISORDERS

SETTING THE SCENE

Historically, services for the emotionally ill and disabled have ranged from utter disregard and denial, and cruel and inhumane treatment, to the more enlightened present-day conditions. For centuries the emotionally ill were scorned and persecuted as pariahs of society, expelled from towns, pilloried and exhibited publicly, jailed as criminals, and sometimes even burned at the stake as witches. These cruel acts were tolerated by an uneducated populace that believed the mentally ill to be possessed of evil spirits and beyond rehabilitation. Early asylums were dungeon-like institutions in which inmates were often chained and locked in cells. Asylum misery often ended in death from the combined effects of malnutrition, disease, and brutal treatment.

Conditions in caring for the emotionally ill were no different in the United States than elsewhere until the mid-nineteenth century. At that time more humane mental hospitals were founded and a change in society's attitude toward the mentally ill slowly began to emerge. Even so, most of those committed to mental hospitals were considered to be incurable and, consequently, were doomed to a lifelong existence as "the living dead."

It was not until well into the twentieth century, that society's perceptions of emotional illness shifted significantly and became more humane. In one turning point, the Vocational Rehabilitation Act of 1943 made the emotionally ill eligible to receive rehabilitation services, representing a major indication of society's change. Combined with the subsequent advent of chemotherapy, admission into the federal-state rehabilitation program signaled a new, enlightened attitude toward emotional disability and led to the freeing of tens of thousands of patients from institutional residences. Though far more positive than in the past, society's attitudes toward mental illness still deter rehabilitation success and deny full opportunities for independent and meaningful living to members of this group.

This chapter offers a broad view of the problems encountered in working with the seriously emotionally disabled, and of ways of dealing with these problems in rehabilitation. It stresses the human, interpersonal aspect of the counselor-client relationship; the need to understand, to communicate, and to reach out actively to motivate the mentally ill to begin the long journey back to their homes and communities. As the author points out, even the most withdrawn patients are conscious of life around them and appreciate those who show concern for their needs. Counseling the emotionally ill involves more than theory and technique, it also requires caring for the person served in a humane way and expressing an abiding faith in the rehabilitation potential of individuals with serious emotional disabilities.

CHAPTER VIII

REHABILITATION OF PERSONS WITH SERIOUS EMOTIONAL DISORDERS

CELIA BENNEY

Concern for the vocational rehabilitation of people with emotional disabilities has steadily mounted in the last two decades and brought with it an avalanche of experimentation and descriptive literature. In considering this body of literature, this chapter will address itself primarily to the implications of findings for vocational rehabilitation in terms of (1) service goals, (2) assessment of clients, and (3) selected aspects of counseling techniques and other types of intervention. The range of emotional disorders is broad, encompassing disabling neuroses, organic syndromes, and major psychoses. The common characteristic of the conditions discussed in the materials that follow is that they disable the person in such important life functions as education and employment.

Attempts to define emotional disabilities lead to questions of what is "normal" and what is "abnormal," and to struggles with classification of the kinds and degrees of severity of behavior disorders. To begin with, there is no universally accepted concept of normality. Some of the difficulties in formulating such a concept were summarized by Maslow and Mittelman (1941) as follows:

(1) Normality is always relative to the particular culture or subculture in which persons live, and to their status, age, sex, and type of personality.

(2) It is difficult to describe the personality objectively without reference to values, ideals, or political and social beliefs.

137

(3) There is no clear line between the normal and the abnormal; and there are many kinds of normality.

(4) Much of what we know about the normal is obtained by extrapolation from the abnormal, and so may be inaccurate.

Maslow and Mittelman viewed abnormality or psychic illness as a set of symptoms that represent a disturbance in some aspect of an individual's functioning. These symptoms are objectively observable, cause subjective suffering, and are considered by the members of a particular society as constituting a definable entity. Such symptoms become part of most people's characteristic behavior and, in time, distinguish them as an individual. By contrast, "normal" individuals lack symptoms of disturbed functioning and adequately satisfy their needs without recourse to "unusual" behaviors.

Rehabilitation workers are placing a lessening emphasis on nosological classification of emotional illness, focusing instead on clients' residual ego strengths and capabilities, helping reduce their sense of fragmentation and regain a feeling of control and power. For those who have had a serious ego breakdown, the counselor may help them recognize perceptual and reality distortions. Selection of a work and social setting in which satisfactory functioning is possible, despite the client's symptoms, may be crucial elements in the rehabilitation process.

People with serious emotional disabilities are confronted by serious vocational adjustment problems in an era of high unemployment. Many are being discharged from institutions without adequate follow-through services in the community and without ready access to adequate housing, training, employment, and recreation. Owing to their limited capacities and employment opportunities they are faced with the discouraging prospect of reentering or entering the labor market at minimal entry level salaries and perhaps find themselves deprived of some of the benefits of governmental support in one form or another. In time, some begin to prefer the security of hospital living to remaining in the community where they may reside in deteriorated buildings and neighborhoods and in an environment that values them minimally.

Assessment

Since employment is a central vocational rehabilitation objective for the emotionally disabled, the following work-related options should be considered in the total assessment of the mental health client:

 (1)   Full or part-time competitive employment
 (2)   Full or part-time school or college attendance
 (3)   Homemaker
 (4)   Sheltered shop employment
 (5)   Volunteer activity
 (6)   Social/recreational participation in the unsheltered community
 (7)   Day hospital and day care groups
 (8)   Half-way house residence
 (9)   Home employment
(10)   Institutional employment

Each of these outcomes is more suitable for some clients than for others. Thus, the selection of appropriate vocational goals is a hoped-for outcome of an assessment process. In arriving at career choice decisions with the client, the counselor usually reviews a wide range of rehabilitation variables, including ego strength, family supports, community resources, and residual capacities.

An appraisal of *ego strengths* includes a consideration of:

(1)   *Pre-illness school and work achievements.* It has been noted that, generally, a good work history is a positive indicator of post-treatment employment. For young people who have never worked, school achievement tends to be a similarly positive prognostic factor. On the other hand, a man of thirty-nine, for example, who graduated from college but did nothing meaningful with his education in the ensuing years, has poor possibilities, even though he may currently have few symptoms and a high I.Q.

(2)   *Amount of ego energy available for vocational purposes.* If work and vocational activity can be undertaken with little interpersonal

conflict, the vocational rehabilitation outlook may be favorable despite remaining behavioral symptoms. In everyday life, some people with psychoses may be habit-trained to exclude their hallucinations from expression on the job site, encapsulating the illness and reducing interpersonal problems in employment.

(3) *Capacity for relationships.* Vocational rehabilitation gain is more likely where there is a history of sustained meaningful relationships and where persons other than professionals currently care about the individual. Although such a relationship may appear tenuous and limited to the external observer, it often has significant implications for most individuals' vocational rehabilitation in that it supports them during customary on-the-job problems and frustrations.

(4) *The meaning of work to the client.* In addition to the usual rehabilitation concerns about the significance of work for an individual in working with emotionally disabled clients, a counselor should be concerned about whether vocational involvement will heighten or reduce anxiety and other symptoms of emotional disorder.

(5) *The capacity of the individual to handle aggressive impulses.* With the emergence of chemotherapy, acting-out behavior has become less common in job situations. However, even today, some emotionally disabled clients do decompensate because of discontinuance of their medication (without anyone knowing it), so that aggressive impulses surface and again become a serious work adjustment problem.

(6) *The client's ego ideals.* The role models selected by clients often influence how they will adapt to a rehabilitation program. In identifying with antisocial, criminal groups, clients become less responsive to rehabilitation. On the other hand, although more positive reference groups have their problems too, they are more supportive of constructive vocational goals and processes.

Family resources and identification are another critical area that should be assessed in service to emotionally disabled clients, including such areas as: (1) *Existence of a functional family and family role in the treatment process.* With all its potential contributions to sustaining mental illness such as double bind messages, seductive parents, intergenerational conflict, and emotionally fragile members, the family can often be helped to become positive facilitators of rehabilitation. At the very least, an interested family can help mitigate loneliness, can supervise medication for the more seriously disturbed clients, and can be available at times when professionals are not, thus enhancing the realization of the clients' rehabilitation potential.

(2) Although family pathology may be of such a nature that separation from the home is necessary, even under these conditions it is often a plus to have a family that can carry some responsibility and offer a place of refuge in crises.

The patient's community should be assessed in vocational rehabilitation in terms of:

(1) *The medical supervision that is available.* The vital role of medication in the treatment and rehabilitation of the mentally ill mandates easy client access to psychiatric supervision of the type and dosage of prescribed medications and medical participation in all aspects of rehabilitation planning.

(2) *Halfway houses or transitional residential facilities.* For clients who cannot live with their families such facilities often provide a stable place in the social environment and access to such essential services as supervision of medication, continuing observation, and a structured, therapeutic milieu.

(3) *Available rehabilitation facilities.* A desirable range of rehabilitation facilities includes: (a) community based sheltered workshops that offer professional services as well as evaluation, work adjustment, skill training and long-term employment; (b) activity programs for leisure hours; (c) work for pay programs having differing degrees of shelter and protection; and (d) work activity centers for clients with limited vocational capacities. Unfortunately, this programming combination does not exist in most communities.

(4) *Linkages between facilities.* Transition points often are crucial in rehabilitating emotionally disabled persons who receive concurrent or sequential services from the school, doctor, workshop, social service facility, and residence, among others. The extent to which these transitions can be planned and managed influences how clients cope with the demands and standards of a variety of helping groups.

In serving emotionally disabled persons, the assessment process as planned by a counselor or case coordinator, regardless of discipline, usually involves a variety of team members. Assessment often begins with history-taking since a key to understanding present behavior often lies in past events. History data may be obtained from institutional records, community case files, family interviews, the clients themselves, and other workers who have interacted with them. While some professionals deemphasize the need for history-taking, it is generally acknowledged that an awareness of an individual's past crises, hospitalizations, acting-out behavior, triggering episodes, relationships with authority figures, and other experiences expedites rehabilitation planning.

Psychological testing is another major source of evaluative information, offering useful clues to areas of competence and conflict, possible organic dysfunction, productivity, and personality, including emotional controls, ego strength, tolerance for frustration, depressive, and other psychological states. Those reports that stress scores and measurements without relating them to behavior and general functioning are of little value to the rehabilitation team. In the history-taking area, it is well to remember that a test experience can be threatening to clients with emotional problems, especially those with paranoid ideation. Thus, careful preparation and support should be provided before a referral for testing is arranged.

Psychiatric interviews, medical examinations, family and social evaluations, and sheltered workshop participation are other types of assessment often used by rehabilitation agencies working with the emotionally disturbed. In a workshop, the manner in which clients interact with their fellow workers, relate to supervision, follow instructions, and generally conduct themselves in a work setting often suggest the clients' contacts with reality, their work personality, and their responsiveness to change.

Rehabilitation Counseling Practices

Micek and Bitter (1974) listed thirteen types of individual psychotherapeutic techniques, five types of institutional therapies, five pharmaceutical and physical therapeutic modalities, three group techniques, and two community-oriented approaches utilized in the rehabilitation of mentally ill individuals. These interventions were:

Individual psychotherapeutic techniques:

   (1)   gestalt therapy
   (2)   reality therapy
   (3)   pastoral counseling
   (4)   existential therapy
   (5)   hypnosis
   (6)   behavior therapy
   (7)   crisis intervention
   (8)   videotape
   (9)   telephone therapy
(10)   art therapy
(11)   music therapy
(12)   poetry
(13)   drama

Institutional therapies:

(1)   milieu therapy and therapeutic community living:

     (a)   work therapy (industrial), sheltered workshop, and protective hospital employment
     (b)   psychodrama
     (c)   family therapy
     (d)   occupational therapy
     (e)   recreational therapy

(2)   Halfway houses, cooperative apartments, and simulated community living
(3)   behavior modification, operant conditioning, and token economy programs
(4)   relationship therapy
(5)   dance therapy

Pharmacotherapy and physical modalities:

(1)   LSD in psychiatric therapy
(2)   Lithium carbonate therapy
(3)   other treatment drugs
(4)   electroconvulsive therapy (bilateral and unilateral)
(5)   electrosleep therapy

Group techniques:

(1)   group therapy, encounter groups, and marathon group therapy
(2)   peer group programs
(3)   transactional analysis

Community-oriented approaches:

(1)   group living in the community
(2)   social clubs and multiagency therapeutic social clubs

Space limitations preclude a discussion of these interventions in this chapter. For more detailed information the reader is referred to Micek and Bitter, and other selected counseling and psychotherapy texts.

Though the prescription of medication for emotionally ill patients is the exclusive province of the physician, the increasing importance of this treatment in rehabilitation requires that counselors gain some knowledge of the drugs used and their effects on client behavior. Professional workers and clients should know chemotherapeutic drugs may render some clients groggy, psychomotorically depressed, and listless; tranquilizers (phenothiazenes) can be dangerous when mixed with alcohol; and side affects and mood changes may be caused by drug use. Unless counselors are aware of these conditions, they may misinterpret client behavior and plan improperly with them. Similarly, a client's performance on a psychological test battery can be strongly influenced by medication. Indeed, when test results appear disparate from observed behavior, one of the first areas counselors should explore is the medication regimen. Finally, in a rehabilitation center, professional staff members may have responsibility to see to it that clients are taking their prescribed medications. Fear of loss of control, or the process of decompensation may cause some clients to fail to take prescribed drugs in the requisite dosage at the times stipulated by their physicians. When this occurs, they may be asked to bring their medication to the rehabilitation facility where intake can be supervised.

There are many psychosocial elements to be considered in providing rehabilitation services to the emotionally disturbed. A primary one is the identification of an appropriate type of service for a client. Too often the selection of a service or facility is not based on what is best for the client, but on convenience factors or the professional worker's bias. An example of this is the restricted use of a sheltered workshop as a rehabilitative facility, that is, making a referral to such a shop only when other treatment modalities have failed or automatically refraining from using a workshop with individuals who have a high I.Q. score or a past history that suggests that a shop experience would be demeaning. In both instances, the worker's assumptions may be incorrect. On the other hand, individuals who are too disturbed, depressed, or unmotivated at a given time may not find the workshop regimen therapeutic and, in fact, may even regress because of shop pressure to conform to rules and practices beyond their capability. Bright clients, with whom a middle-class-oriented, college-educated staff sometimes overidentifies, may be considered ready for further education, skilled training, or even competitive employment too soon, when actually they are very anxious and threatened by entry into such demanding assignments. Attending a workshop and working at simple tasks for a period of time may often be helpful in enhancing self-confidence and ego strength.

Persons with serious emotional problems can be impeded in their rehabilitation programs by their inability to use available public transportation, especially in the earlier stages. As clients progress in the rehabilitation program and become more independent in travel activities, they tend to require less transportation assistance, but at the point that they desire it their need is as compelling as that of the physically handicapped. Some institutionalized persons seem to be neglected in institutions because it is assumed, sometimes erroneously, that they are never going to be able to function in the community. Some of the residents are fearful of the world outside and cannot take the next step toward greater independence unless helping staff members go beyond immediate caretaking services and offer rehabilitation assistance. Included in this assistance is counseling and training designed to help them to overcome their fears and prepare for community living. Staff support from referring institutions as well as from workshop personnel is also necessary as clients begin workshop programs. Counselors from both staffs may colead therapy groups until such time as initial anxieties are alleviated. Staff helping behavior sometimes is mistakenly interpreted as fostering dependence when, in fact, opposite results are achieved.

Client motivation is a major concern in vocational rehabilitation. As with other disability groups, positive employment motivation is a sine qua non of the vocational rehabilitation process. Without motivation, even good work skills do not assure employment success. However many severely emotionally disabled individuals, especially those with chronic schizophrenia, often come to rehabilitation facilities appearing withdrawn, hopeless, helpless, lacking interest in people, and with little commitment to work, in other words, totally unmotivated. To quote Emily Dickinson, they seem to be saying "I'm nobody! Who are You? Are you nobody too?" Caught between the crossfire of their desire to withdraw and their need for human contact, their concomitant wish for independence and merger with a helping person, their fear of closeness and their concurrent intense loneliness, their passivity, and, at other times, their aggressive push, they are often emotionally "stuck" rather than motivated. Sometimes, they cannot even mobilize themselves to take the first steps along the rehabilitation road. The fear of success may be as overwhelming as the fear of failure. Some may have all their energies focused on maintaining defenses in the face of total personality disorganization, while others may not. From this, it can be seen how difficult it is to characterize this client group of emotionally disabled individuals.

Perhaps the most distinguishing, obvious, and important characteristic of people with chronic schizophrenia is the breakdown of ego boundaries with attendant thought disorders—primary process thinking, inability to distinguish between inner and outer phenomena, feelings of depersonalization, confusion of identity, hallucinations, delusions, loss of a sense of continuity and time, and so forth. Even these symptoms are not universally present or omnipresent. However, it is well to remember that as serious and all-encompassing as schizophrenia is, it is only one of the numerous emotional disorders that bring clients into rehabilitation.

In working with the emotionally disabled, it is the counselor's task to motivate the clients to ultimately assume responsibility for themselves. Unfortunately there is no universal formula for establishing a connection with another human being, but this much is known. Counselors must care, be open, honest, and authentic. If they are not, the client will quickly know it. Empathetic understanding can be expressed in many ways, some of them nonverbal, but, in all instances, some form of communication is a requisite. Frieda Fromm Reichman described an interaction with a mute schizophrenic patient who had come to her office several times and been unable to talk with her. Finally, one day he came in and held up his forefinger (the rest of his hand was closed). Recognizing the patient's deep loneliness, her response was "All alone?," thus establishing contact. Some disturbed clients who cannot verbalize can express feelings through writing. On the other hand, just touching may reach someone and indicate concern. Additional motivational techniques include situational support, such as supplying subway tokens, or providing coins for other purposes when clients are not considered ready to handle money, as well as other concrete measures that help them develop a feeling of mastery over their environment. Another important involvement technique is that of assigning counselors to clients according to personality, sex, or orientation in accordance with clients' needs. Challenging clients and jarring them out of set, sick patterns is sometimes an effective way of reaching them. Once a working relationship has been established, Frank (1973) feels that one of the conditions for successful psychotherapy is established. Other ingredients making for successful therapy include a therapeutic setting, and a therapeutic rationale linked to certain specific procedures.

In counseling emotionally disabled people it is especially important for workers to maintain a high degree of self-awareness because clients are perceptive in this area, and cue into the counselor's feelings with great accuracy. If a counselor is intensely anxious, fearful, or angry —and who isn't at times—in the presence of certain clients, it is helpful to be able to acknowledge these feelings to yourself and perhaps even to them in order to determine whether such feelings are elicited by a whole category of clients or only selected individuals, and to be able to cope with the emotions that appear. Countertransference can play havoc with clients whether it be positive or negative. The self-awareness of a counselor also relates to hearing what clients are saying, beyond their overt verbalizations. Some clients may declare that they wish to go to school or work, but then break all their appointments or react with an exacerbation of symptoms, that is, intense immobilizing anxiety or recurrent hallucinations when confronted by work or school situations. Listening to and hearing the moods of the emotionally disabled clients are of utmost importance since their reactions are highly significant, though not always visible.

A client's history is of great importance in alerting workers to those conditions which tend to trigger suicidal gestures or acts. The counselor-client relationship is primary in freeing the client to talk about self-destructive thoughts. It is a myth that asking clients if they have such thoughts precipitates suicide. Counselors, family members, and psychiatrists should be alerted to suicidal threats, and appropriate arrangements should be made, depending upon psychiatric advice, that is, increased supervision at home, hospitalization, change of medication, and so forth. Anniversary dates of loss of significant people and holidays are often periods requiring special attention. Fantasies of reunion with a deceased parent or relative are to be treated seriously. Any separation, such as vacations of therapists or counselors, may stimulate deep depression in already fragile people.

In recent years group counseling has become one of the primary rehabilitation modalities for the emotionally disabled. The group approach helps clients to identify problems, strengthen egos by means of confrontation and other interaction techniques, elevate social functioning, mitigate feelings of loneliness, decrease one's sense of helplessness while enhancing independence, expose oneself to feedback that improves self-perception, and reinforces realistic behavior. Rehabilitation group approaches embody similar positive possibilities for the emotionally disabled client.

The Rehabilitation Workshop

The physical industrial-like features of a rehabilitation workshop sometimes arouse quite negative feelings in mental health professionals. Some think that a workshop is a drab, depressing setting where clients perform "meaningless" or demeaning work activities. Concomitantly, many of them are unaware of the variety of services and programs offered by modern workshops, such as the "caring" attitudes of the staff, the respect conveyed to clients, the emphasis on strengths rather than the sickness of the clients, and the readiness to anticipate and respond to interpersonal conflicts. In addition to activities directed toward the development of a work personality, workshops usually offer individual and group counseling, recreational and social activities, and adult education classes, all planned to meet a client's intellectual, social, and emotional needs.

A rehabilitation workshop provides unique opportunities for reality testing. For one thing, there is the structured nature of productive work activity that requires appropriate productive behavior. When a job is performed poorly, a supervisor is present to correct and instruct the client, and when it is well done the appropriate behavior is reinforced by praise and tangible rewards. Earning and handling money offer opportunities for enhancing responsible and independent functioning. In fact, the experience of being dealt with as a worker, rather than a patient, is in itself therapeutic.

Since most work opportunities involve contact with others, the workshop can provide some reconditioning or desensitization (in behavioral terms) relative to interaction with others. Inappropriate reactions not only to peers, but supervisors, can be observed and, hopefully, handled. Some interpersonal problems that manifest themselves in the work setting can be further dealt with in activity-oriented individual or group counseling in a much more realistic way.

Regressed individuals are often quite unaware of how they dress or appear, partly as a result of earlier institutionalization experiences, and also because of low self-esteem. The work setting is a good milieu in which clients can learn how to dress and care for themselves appropriately in a context of expectations of "normal" appearance and behavior. Workshops are also useful in structuring time for emotionally ill persons who lack the ability to use time constructively. Thus, interacting with the requirements of the work setting becomes an educational experience in reorienting clients to the demands of time.

Job Placement

Problems in finding employment are plentiful even for those emotionally disabled clients who are fully ready for a job. Questions that should be considered by counselors when considering placement are:

(1) Should the client reveal his illness to prospective employers? (2) Can the client tolerate the pressures of a particular job, does he or she need special supervision, can he or she work with males and females, and are there on-the-job interpersonal demands that will create excessive stress? (3) Does a particular job represent a vocational upgrading or downgrading, and does this meet the client's needs and interests at this time?

Both the client and the rehabilitation counselor often are confronted with the dilemma of whether to reveal a history of mental illness to a prospective employer. In some cases the client has no choice. Firms that do routine preemployment physical examinations, including urinalysis, will probably note the presence of drugs used to treat an emotional illness. Large companies whose employees must be bonded will probably gain access to information regarding previous hospitalizations for emotional illness. Some agencies, both voluntary and public, have a policy of informing employers of past emotional illness. Indeed, some clients experience excessive guilt and anxiety if they withhold telling an employer. For them the fear of being "found out" is greater than the fear of being denied a job.

In some instances there is an advantage to the client in informing an employer of former illness. A few companies actually contribute to the cost of an employee's psychotherapy, and some assist in the rehabilitation process by treating job requirements flexibly while a client gains in ego strength. However, these are rare cases compared with the incidence of employer prejudice and job discrimination displayed by the great majority of firms toward former mental patients. In actuality, there often is no more need to inform an employer of an emotional illness than of a physical disability, and clients who choose not to do so should have their decision respected by counselors. Too often counselors assisting a client in preparing a résumé, or in readying for an interview, are more concerned with their reputations and own sense of values than with the client's vocational needs.

The level of the proposed job is another difficult placement problem faced by clients and counselors. Some emotional disabilities are cyclical, some reversible, and some progressive, necessitating a differential approach to job placement. Experience has shown that while some clients require a job that is less challenging than the one previously held, others acquire new skills and strengths in the rehabilitation process and can enter more skilled work than was possible in the past.

What must be determined is the client's *current* capacities and needs, rather than being locked into previous educational or vocational experiences. As clients achieve success with immediate tasks they may be able to develop realistically higher aspirations. Thus, career development for these clients can be seen as a stairway, to be mastered a step at a time.

A Case History

Mrs. T., a young woman of twenty-five, when initially referred to a rehabilitation center, could not be immediately accepted because she was acutely disturbed, intensely hostile, delusional about her husband's supposed homosexual adultery, and unwilling to take medication because not taking it was evidence that she was less sick.

The first intervention necessary was to make medication a condition of acceptance at the rehabilitation workshop. The client agreed, since life at home was intolerable. She described an intense sado-masochistic relationship with her husband involving assaultive and violent behavior. In the course of this relationship, she had abdicated responsibility for her three-year-old son to her mother.

The client's history revealed a traumatic background of family disorganization, movement back and forth between the homes of her parents, both of whom had remarried, and temporary placement with relatives. Medically she had a history of two hospitalizations for rheumatic fever as a child, was on the critical list both times, and had suffered panic reactions because no one explained painful treatment procedures or told her what was wrong.

On the positive side, she had high average to superior intelligence and artistic ability, had completed one year in college, and had held jobs, though these were short-term and on a low-skill level. She was admitted to the workshop after demonstrating that she could retain contact with the psychiatrist.

During the course of the next year she was able to complete training as a clerk typist, with the aid of many supports and active interventions provided by the counselor. Concretely, she needed financial help from time to time with necessities such as medication and transportation, until she could be helped to obtain welfare assistance, sponsorship by the Office of Vocational Rehabilitation, and money for knitting supplies to mitigate her loneliness after she arranged separation from her husband. She was also given financial aid for other forms of recreation and clothing to help enhance her self-esteem. In time, she was able to move closer to her child and permit herself to feel some warmth and love in that relationship. In this framework, the counselor gave direct advice about child rearing, particularly after the birth of the second child (which occurred during the period of rehabilitation).

Initially the client had had intense, ambivalent feelings toward the counselor, which were so frightening to her that interviews were kept short and, on some occasions, had to be held in the large open space of the cafeteria to dilute the feeling of closeness and fears of introjection. Although at times she had intellectual insight into her projections, emotionally she initially believed that her stepfather, husband, and sister wanted to kill her.

The client's self-defeating behavior was manifested in her early experience at the workshop by very poor work and daydreaming. When confronted with the reality of her performance, she was ready to run away. The counselor clearly and firmly let her know that this had been her previous behavior in job situations and that her counselor would not "permit her to get away with this." She was able to respond to the counselor's message of hope and conviction, to reveal that she had gone off medication, and subsequently resumed taking it. Subsequently, the medication was supervised by the nurse at the workshop. The counselor clearly indicated that she expected Mrs. T. to be able to attain the goal of working in competitive industry but that she could move toward that goal at her own pace.

Mrs. T. spent many sessions discussing her hostile feelings and her ambivalence toward the counselor, who she both liked and feared. On one occasion she had an anxiety reaction in relation to this during which she noticed that the counselor was reacting and asked whether the counselor was nervous. The counselor told her that she was reacting to her anxiety and the client then was able to talk about her feelings of ambivalence toward the worker which were producing the anxiety.

Gradually, as she was able to discuss the severe beatings she had suffered from her father and stepfather, she gained some awareness of the hostility that resulted from this as well as the fact that love and closeness became equated for her with brutality. As she was able to engage in a corrective relationship with a strong female counselor (her own mother was rather helpless and passive), she began to move toward other people and to have some social life. She also used a group experience at the workshop to gain some awareness of how she kept herself away from people while wanting very much to relate to them. She made friends at the workshop and was able to engage in off-the-job activities with them.

For a brief period, with the approval of her psychiatrist, she resumed contact with her husband, became pregnant, and admitted that she wanted the baby because she desired to have someone close to her whom she could love. Symbolically, she felt that the child was herself and she wanted to be reborn and start life all over again. As might be expected, the relationship with her husband was short-lived. In spite of the pregnancy she continued her training almost to the point of delivery, and was quite ready for employment by that time. She needed considerable help with the arrangements for the care of her children but was able to make these satisfactorily and to secure a job which offered possibilities of growth and advancement.

There were periods during her rehabilitation when there were exacerbations of her illness and she had many distorted perceptions of the counselor and others. One time this was handled by the counselor insisting on direct, in-person contact rather than by telephone calls, so that the distortions could be dealt with more directly. It should be noted that the workshop supervisor was also an extremely supportive person in that she was able to convey warmth and keep sufficient distance at the same time, as well as to teach necessary work skills. Mrs. T. learned much about what she did to provoke abuse from others and this awareness carried over into the job situation.

At the end of two years, she was employed, was able to enjoy her children, had an ongoing but distant relationship with a man, and was continuing under psychiatric care. Her mother summed up the situation by telling the counselor that she felt Mrs. T. might have spent her life in a hospital if it were not for the agency's interventions and rehabilitation program.

Summary

The major consideration in the rehabilitation of people with emotional disabilities is the recognition by the worker that there are innumerable variables which can affect programming for this group.

Among these variables are society's view of the disorder, social resources and trends, and counselor skill. Much of this skill can be
acquired so that rehabilitation work with this group becomes a science
as well as an art. The effective counselor who works in a high emotional
demand situation should be prepared to cope with multiple aspects of
their clients, their families, and the communities, skillfully orchestrat-
ing them all to arrive at the most effective program for each individual.

BIBLIOGRAPHY

Beck, Alan T. M.D. *Depression.* Philadelphia: University of Pennsylvania
    Press, 1970.
Benney, Celia, M.S.S. "Factors Affecting Motivation for Rehabilitation,"
    reprinted from *The Psychiatric Quarterly Supplement,* Vol. 38, Part 2, 1964.
Boszormenyi-Nagy, I. M.D. and Framo, J. L., Ph.D. eds. *Intensive Family
    Therapy.* New York: Harper & Row, 1965.
Bryce, L., Boyer, M.D. and Giovacchini, Peter L., M.D. *Psychoanalytical
    Treatment of Schizophrenic and Characterological Disorders.* New York: Science
    House, 1967.
Federn, Paul. *Ego Psychology and the Psychoses.* New York: Basic Books, 1952.
Frank, Jerome D., M.D. *Current Psychiatric Therapies.* Jules H. Masserman,
    M.D. ed. New York: Grune & Stratton, Vol. 13, 1973.
Frank, J. D. "Reorientation-Psychotherapy or Psychotherapies," Jules H.
    Masserman, ed., *Current Psychiatric Therapies,* 1973, vol. 13, p. 19.
Freeman, Cameron and McGhee. *Chronic Schizophrenia.* New York: Interna-
    tional Universities Press, 1973.
Hartmann, Heinz. *Ego Psychology and the Problems of Adaptation.* New York:
    International Universities Press, 1958.
Hawrylick, Alex. "Rehabilitation Gain. A New Criterion for An Old Con-
    cept," *Rehabilitation Literature,* November 1974, vol. 35, no. 11.
Health Services and Mental Health Administration, U.S. Department
    of Health, Education, and Welfare. "A Demonstration in Rehabilitation
    of the Mentally Ill Adolescent & Young Adult." Contract Number MH
    1036-2
Laing, R. D. *Politics of Experience.* New York: Pantheon Books, 1967.
Laing, R. D. and Easterson. *Sanity and Madness and the Family,* 2nd ed. New
    York: Basic Books Inc., 1971.

Lidz, T., Fleck, S., and Cornelison, A. *Schizophrenia and the Family*. New York: International Universities Press, 1965.

Maslow, A. H. and Mittleman, B. *Principles of Abnormal Psychology*. New York: Harper and Brothers, 1941, pp. 26-45.

Menninger, Karl, M.D. *The Vital Balance*. New York: Viking Press, 1963.

Micek, L. A. and Bitter, J. A. "Service Delivery Approaches for Difficult Rehabilitation Clients," Rehabilitation Literature, September 1974, vol. 35, no. 9, p. 258.

Fromm Reichman, Frieda. *Principles of Intensive Psychotherapy*. Chicago: University of Chicago Press, 1950.

Schlesinger, Benno. *Higher Cerebral Functions and Their Clinical Disorders*, in Spotnitz, M.D., *Modern Psychoanalysis of the Schizophrenic Patient*. New York: Grune & Stratton, 1962.

Searles, Harold F. *Collected Papers on Schizophrenia and Related Subjects*. New York: International Universities Press, 1965.

Sullivan, H. S., M.D. *Schizophrenia As A Human Process*. New York: W. Norton & Co., 1963.

Yalon, Irving D. *The Theory & Practice of Group Psychotherapy*. New York: Basic Books, 1970.

IMPLICATIONS FOR REHABILITATION PRACTICE

Increased service experience with emotionally disabled clients has led rehabilitation workers to place less emphasis on nosological classifications of mental illness and more on functional potential. In this framework a rehabilitation evaluation should provide information about residual ego strengths and individual learning styles. In order to assess these, counselors should examine a client's work history, educational experience, and family and social relationships, as well as using customary conventional evaluation tools such as psychological and work sample testing.

Individual and group techniques are among the large number of interventions used with the emotionally disabled. The use of chemotherapy has gained increasing importance in reducing symptoms, and counselors may have to supervise clients taking their medication. Additional knowledge of any drugs used is required for an understanding of the effects of such drugs on client behavior. As in the case of

chemotherapy counselors are being required to understand and work
with many new and sometimes dramatic interventions.

While client motivation is a major concern in service to all disability
groups, it is of special significance for the emotionally disabled.
Members of this group often appear withdrawn, hopeless, helpless,
lacking interest in people and with little commitment to work. Despite
their withdrawn, self-oriented behavior these clients are aware of their
surroundings and know whether counselors care for them and are open
and authentic. Communication is difficult and often takes nonverbal
forms to establish contact. Clients may express a desire to attend a
workshop or a class and then break appointments and find excuses for
not meeting their commitments. In this disability, more than in others,
counselors must be sensitive to client moods and disguised meanings.

The role of the rehabilitation workshop is misunderstood by many
mental health professionals who regard it as a drab, depressing setting
where clients perform demeaning tasks. These professionals lack an
understanding of the therapeutic nature of work, and the unique
opportunities for reality testing at the shop. The experience of being
dealt with as an employee, rather than a patient, earning and handling
money, and working toward the satisfaction of needs, may be as therapeutic for emotionally disabled clients as any other intervention.

When clients are finally ready for job placement, they are faced with
the dilemma of whether to reveal their history as a mental patient to a
prospective employer. In some cases where physical examinations are
given or employees must be bonded there is no choice. But at other
times clients may decide not to tell, and this choice must be respected
by counselors who should be more concerned with the client's vocational needs than with their own reputations and sense of values.

CHAPTER IX

COUNSELING THE MENTALLY RETARDED

SETTING THE SCENE

Over the years the meaning of the term retardation has been greatly broadened and changed. Originally it was descriptive of a small group of people who were born with severe intellectual deficits and who, mostly, ended up in institutions where they were cared for the rest of their lives. As our society developed and schools increasingly used intelligence and other tests for educational decisions, the retardation classification was applied to all those persons who scored below stipulated levels on such instruments. This now encompassed a much larger population of individuals with a wide variety of physical, emotional, and cultural disabilities whose only similarity was that they performed relatively poorly on intelligence tests. In those days retarded persons tended to be lumped together and treated undifferentially in special classes where they received attenuated educations and were isolated socially from peers. After leaving school, they were sent to sheltered workshops where their potential generally was underestimated by rehabilitation personnel as it had been by educators.

In recent years greater attention has been paid to the process of subnormal functioning so that appropriate methods of assisting retarded individuals could be prescribed differentially according to individual learning capacities. Basic to all else in avoidance of stereotyping those considered retarded is to concentrate on functional potential. This chapter discusses the complex nature of retardation and how counseling may be used more effectively to foster the development of retarded clients. It points out that currently counselors limit their approach to retarded clients to rigid systems that grossly underestimate the many educational and vocational possibilities that are open to retarded persons in American society.

159

CHAPTER IX

COUNSELING THE MENTALLY RETARDED

David Malikin and Herbert Rusalem

The definition of mental retardation has been a serious concern of physicians, psychologists, psychiatrists, educators, and social workers for many years. Numerous organic, social, behavioral, and intellectual aspects of retardation have been specified in varying degrees as contributors to a condition that is fairly well recognized in professional practice but which still defies precise universal definition. For some period of time, almost total reliance was placed upon cutoff scores on individual intelligence tests of one sort or another. Subsequently, a more functional view began to prevail which stresses client capabilities in meeting the demands of everyday living at least as much as the findings of formal standardized measures (Allen and Cortazzo, 1970). Even today, however, full agreement on a definition of mental retardation is lacking and the process of formulation goes on. Obviously, the subsequent emergence of a consensus definition satisfactory to all will have value for workers in this field, but from a rehabilitation viewpoint definition is not the essential problem in the mounting of improved programs. Names and categories have never been indispensable in enlightened rehabilitation practice. Indeed, most rehabilitation workers are aware that terminology has a vital legal and administrative connotation in setting boundaries for eligibility. However, once actual client service begins, the implications of the label are less cogent. In fact, to the degree that definitions foster clinical stereotypes and generalized treatment modes keyed to rigid, nosological constructs, they may be more of a barrier than a facilitator to the rehabilitation of mentally retarded individuals.

The central concept of mental retardation that should concern rehabilitation workers is that, on specified academic and learning tasks, a client deviates from the general population to such an extent that his/her progress toward independent employment is likely to be delayed or impeded to such a degree that special rehabilitation interventions are required. In actuality, the consequences of mental retardation are exceedingly diverse. Some mentally retarded persons are limited primarily in some school-related tasks; others at the opposite pole are impeded by their intellectual limitations in almost everything they do. Not uncommonly, the intellectual limitations are highly uneven in their impact upon the person, limiting him more markedly in some types of activities than in others. This uneven pattern differs widely from one mentally retarded person to the next. If the concept of individual differences has relevance for rehabilitation, in general, it is even more relevant for rehabilitation clients who have one or more intellectual deficits that render them less socially or vocationally effective.

As a consequence, rehabilitation workers should not react to the label of mental retardation with prepackaged responses. If a client is eligible for agency service, the counselor need not search for more exact parameters of the retardation but for definitive data concerning actual client functioning. In other words, what a client can or cannot do, or in the terms of the Learning Capacities Research Project (Rusalem and Rusalem, Unpublished) what a client can or cannot learn to do, is far more revealing for rehabilitation programming than test scores, school grades, or subgroupings. Indeed, as the Learning Capacities Research Project (and other investigations) have demonstrated, the usual diagnostic labels tend to obscure rather than illuminate the rehabilitation potential of individuals who have intellectual limitations.

In this context, rehabilitation programming should be initiated only after the level of client functioning in a wide variety of vocationally related activities has been ascertained. A multifaceted evaluation should consist of medical, psychological, learning capacities, work sample, workshop, social service, occupational and physical therapy, therapeutic recreation, and home and family examinations conducted with the major purpose of identifying client strengths and potentialities, rather than losses or deficits. Through this process, unsuspected client resources often emerge because earlier perceptions of the individual were dominated by the apparent retardation. But retardation rarely cuts across all domains of human functioning. Most commonly, retarded persons are more handicapped in certain respects than in others.

Equally important from the rehabilitation perspective is the fact confirmed by the Learning Capacities Research Project that a mental retardation classification often is as much a function of the environment as of the individual. Thus, some retarded clients are very handicapped in school situations but less so in certain out-of-school activities. Furthermore, certain conditions imposed unwittingly in the rehabilitation setting (for example, excessive counselor verbalization, inappropriate vocabulary, improper instructional methods, or demands for innovative problem solving) may render clients more retarded than they might otherwise be (DiMichael, 1964). Conversely, more favorable conditions in a rehabilitation facility may reduce or even eliminate some evidences of retardation.

In the same way that some homebound persons may be rendered nonhomebound, by eliminating architectural barriers, so may some higher level retarded individuals be rendered nonretarded in some situations by structuring the environment differently. Even when retardation cannot be eliminated to any extent by environmental adjustments, such adjustments can elevate functioning level to a vocationally significant extent. This environmental concept of mental retardation rehabilitation applies to the counseling process as well. If the conditions of counseling are compatible with client capacities, then mental retardation need not call for dramatically different counseling approaches. In practice, any counseling system that is suitable for the nonretarded also is suitable for the retarded so long as the demands made upon the individual client are compatible with his or her capacities. This reinforces the need of the rehabilitation worker to have available dependable data on clients' functional abilities, potentialities, and learning capacities. The latter, a new service pioneered by Rusalem and Rusalem, points up learning potential as the most favorable means by which any client can learn various tasks and demonstrate previously unrevealed but highly important resources that he/she may have for entry into training or employment.

The foregoing should not be interpreted as contraindicating existing categories or classifications of mental retardation or of efforts to add precision to current definitions. It does, however, suggest that the crucial variable for the rehabilitation worker is an awareness of what the client might achieve under the most favorable counseling, instructional and other environmental conditions, that can be designed for him/her. In essence, the responsibility of the worker is not so much to focus upon the mentally retarded client's losses as upon the residual strengths, a concept that has been widely accepted for the more than 50 years of vocational rehabilitation history.

The tendency toward individualizing services for mentally retarded rehabilitation clients has been manifested by a broader view of occupational opportunities for this group. Even ten years ago, vocational decision-making by members of this caseload was encumbered by vocational stereotyping which limited them to a relatively small range of occupational choices (Rothstein, 1961). For example, "popular" occupations for the retarded included such standbys as messenger, food service worker, elevator operator, hand assembler, building maintenance worker, low-level helper, and packager. With the development of greater respect for the capacities of retarded persons and more sophisticated evaluation procedures, it is becoming evident that counselors should help clients choose from a far more extensive range of fields, including certain types of machine operation, clerical tasks, personal service, and even skilled trades. Obviously, many occupations will continue to be unfeasible for some mentally retarded persons, but this is as true for the gifted as for the retarded. The important consideration for rehabilitation workers, however, is to resist any pressures exerted upon them to stereotype the occupational choice process for retarded clients and to keep an open mind regarding all fields of work until it becomes clear which are most suitable for the individual client.

The same trend is evident in terms of selecting rehabilitation facilities. Special rehabilitation agencies for the retarded were established because, at that time, retarded persons could not gain ready access to needed rehabilitation services in existing "general" facilities. However, exclusions of this type are less common now than in the past. In selecting a facility for a mentally retarded client, rehabilitation workers should avoid automatic client segregation as much as they avoid automatic vocational choice. In view of their individual capacities, interests, and preferences, some retarded clients might best be served by a facility developed especially for retarded individuals. On the other hand, others may benefit to a greater extent from an experience in a facility in which mentally retarded persons are rehabilitated side-by-side with members of other disability groups.

Research in the field of mental retardation suggests that few, if any, overarching generalizations can be made about all or even most mentally retarded clients concerning personality, vocational interests, social and cultural experiences, and responsivity to rehabilitation. Even in such an extreme situation as that confronting lifelong residents of a state institution for the mentally retarded, the range of human differences is almost infinite. For example, in serving residents of the Willowbrook State School in New York, the Federation of the Handicapped (Rusalem and Cohen, Unpublished) found that attempts to formulate a generalized day center program for a total client group of this type was counterproductive in the light of the vast range of client traits. Despite the numbing effects of institutional living, the tendency of institutions to impose repetitive responses upon their residents, and the long history of denial of individuality, the members of this group (as with any other similar group elsewhere) stubbornly retained their individuality and their sense of identity. In fact, early in this project, these residents manifested a need for highly differential individualized programming. In a few cases, it was found that some of these Willowbrook residents weren't retarded at all according to the customary criteria but had been placed in Willowbrook decades ago for social and psychological reasons that no one can remember today.

The message for rehabilitation workers is clear. Beyond their customary commitment to safeguard the right of every client to respect, dignity, understanding, acceptance, and confidentiality, workers owe mentally retarded clients a concurrent commitment to their differences. Any evaluation, counseling, training, or employment procedure that "shoe-horns" these clients into preconceived categories violates this basic principle. Although rehabilitation workers should learn as much as they can about the implications of mental retardation for vocational rehabilitation processes, the principal thing that they must know is that retardation is not the sole determiner of rehabilitation programs. Once workers begin to use this concept as their guiding frame of reference for offering service to the members of this group, mentally retarded persons will be well on their way toward realizing their rehabilitation potential.

It has long been felt, in some quarters, that orthodox, face-to-face counseling with the mentally retarded is unproductive. Some professionals believe that a limited ability to verbalize and conceptualize prevents retardates from developing insight and expressing themselves

adequately, often key requirements in counseling. This view of retarded persons persists despite the existence of a body of research and
clinical experience indicating that retarded clients can and do benefit
from counseling. Thorne (1948) reported the results of a two-year
intensive counseling program with 30 male and 38 female institutionalized retardates. Consisting mostly of young people, the group had
been referred for counseling because of acting-out and other malad-
justive behavior. Objective and clinical judgments indicated that 45 of
these 68 clients had improved greatly from counseling, 16 remained the
same, and 7 had worsened during the two-year study period. Concluding that counseling with the mentally retarded is both possible
and advantageous, Thorne noted that the most difficult obstacle to
successful counseling was the defeatist attitude of the institutional
staff.

In an even earlier paper Chidester (1934) reported the therapeutic
counseling gain made by three retardates, (a schizophrenic, a neurotic,
and the third with an endocrine disturbance). Though one cannot
generalize from this limited study, it should be noted that along with
other positive changes the I.Q. scores for these individuals rose 10, 19,
and 34 points respectively. This finding helped dispel the then preva-
lent opinion that retardation, regardless of cause, was irreversible.
Other researches by Walsh (1920), Sarason (1944), and DeMartino
(1954) indicated that even psychoanalytic methods could be used in
counseling retardates. These investigators reported that the direct and
undisguised dreams of retardates could be used therapeutically with
them. On the basis of process report accounts drawn from his own
caseload, Browning (1974) noted emotional and social gains of retarded clients involved in an extensive counseling experience. These
included insight formation and behavioral change as part of an improved adjustment to their environments. Additional support for the
counseling of retardates appears in articles by Sternlicht (1966),
Gardner (1971), Heber (1961), and many others. The evidence appears
clear that any bias against counseling with retardates is untenable, and
that with few exceptions they should be given opportunities to participate in this service process.

A useful starting point when counseling a retarded client is to
disregard labels and to focus on residual capacities and abilities. In
adopting this stance, it is well to keep in mind that there are many
organic, emotional, nutritional, environmental, and genetic conditions

that contribute to and complicate subnormal intellectual functioning. This suggests that while some types of retardation may be relatively constant, others are temporary, partially remediable, or reversible. It also implies that diagnosing the functional consequences of retardation and treating clients differentially is essential for successful counseling with this group. Finally, since retarded individuals are very much like the rest of us, it follows that counseling with them will be similar to counseling with other populations, taking into account the special psychosocial, educational, and vocational problems related to intellectual deficits.

A general goal of counseling is to assist people to resolve problems, and in the process learn to cope with subsequent life problems more independently and successfully. Two important assumptions underlie this goal: (1) individuals are aware of their problems, and (2) they voluntarily seek counseling assistance to help them with these problems. In actual practice those clients who share these assumptions, and refer themselves, are better prepared and more motivated for counseling because they have some idea about the problems causing them difficulty, and because right from the start they regard the counselor as someone who can assist them to resolve these problems. By contrast, clients who are referred by others for counseling initially present less favorable attitudes. They often deny knowing the reasons for seeing a counselor, and regard him with suspicion and distrust. Based on past experience, clients referred by others tend to regard counselors as authority figures to be dealt with in a bureaucratic jungle. These remarks are relevant to the retarded because a large majority of them enter counseling with only a partial understanding of why they are there, and accordingly they begin the experience fearfully.

A crucial element of a counselor-client relationship, trust, is a learned response and a central ingredient in the establishment of rapport. Yet, the unfortunate experiences of many retardates, particularly higher level ones, has taught them to be wary and distrustful of strangers. Thus, an essential aspect of counseling with this group is that of helping them to learn to trust another person again. On the other hand, more severely retarded individuals are often childlike in their need to trust adult and authority figures, including counselors. In these cases a dependency type relationship develops in which the "obedient" individual bends to the desires of a parentlike figure, rather than participating in a wholesome, give-and-take counseling relationship. Mentally retarded individuals who have acted out, committed crimes, or in a variety of ways proven difficult to manage, constitute still another subgroup, with lifetime experiences marked by excessive abuse that have taught them that no one is to be trusted, a feeling they bring to the counseling relationship. It can be seen that establishing rapport with these various subgroups of retardates is a complex task for the rehabilitation counselor.

Values, interests, and needs, as explicit concepts, are rarely considered in discussion of counseling with the mentally retarded. Although these concepts are infrequent subjects in counseling any clients, regardless of I.Q. level, because many counselors tend to lack adequate understanding of them, they are even more overlooked in counseling the retarded. For example, in a seven-page index of a well-known book on behavioral counseling (Krumboltz and Thoresen, 1969), the terms values, interests, and needs are not mentioned once. In a judgmental sense, a value is a personal, overarching concept with positive connotations and implications. Since values are individually determined, they vary from person to person. On the other hand, an interest is a feeling of concern, intentness, or curiosity which motivates us to learn more and involve ourselves more fully in an activity, event, or object that is the focus of the interest. For its part, a need is defined as a meaningful or essential desire that requires satisfaction. There are physiological needs, such as for food and water, and also psychological or emotional needs, such as for love or friendship. The importance of values, interests, and needs in human life is that they serve as prime motivators of behavior. Just about everything people do is influenced by values and interests and is aimed toward the satisfaction of needs. This is as true for retarded individuals as for anyone else. Helping a counselee become more aware of, and more active in shaping and controlling personal values, interests, and needs is an important purpose of counseling. This is difficult to accomplish because these concepts are rarely part of conscious thought, and most counselees would find it difficult to articulate them. As may be expected retarded individuals, generally, have even greater difficulty in developing insights about their values, interests, and needs, suggesting a compelling need for skillful counseling.

An equally neglected topic in counseling the mentally retarded is that of the self-concept. As with other abstract topics, counselors frequently assume that a concept of self is insufficiently concrete to be comprehended by anyone of less than average intelligence. Much counseling experience suggests that this is a fallacious notion and that, in fact, many retarded individuals are highly concerned with how they perceive themselves and the degree to which these perceptions differ from how others perceive them. Since social adequacy is one of the prime determiners of a level of adjustment, realistic awareness of self on the part of retarded clients often is a central goal of counseling. Interpersonal skills critical for vocational success are acquired and sustained in a context of self-understanding and self-acceptance. Hence, functional retardates who are more realistically aware of their assets and deficits tend to cope more adequately with rehabilitation and employment challenges. Equally important in serving them is the need to foster self-acceptance as a necessary precondition for accepting others.

The retardate's family plays a central role in the formation of his self-concept and should be, if anything, more frequently involved in the counseling process than the families of other individuals. In some cases, families provide retarded children with love and security and relate to them realistically and positively. In these instances, retarded children are given the opportunity to develop independence and vocational maturity in accordance with their potential. Unfortunately, many family interactions with retarded members are characterized by either stifling overprotection or overt rejection. Overprotective parents tend to regard their retarded children as useless, ineffective individuals unable to do anything for themselves. They are fearful of independent travel, job placement, out of home activities, and unsupervised peer relationships for their young people. Such parents, unintentionally foster dependence, fearfulness, and a negative self-image. At the other extreme, rejecting parents who neglect their retarded offsprings, treat them abusively, and create unstable, chaotic home environments that are emotionally scarring. For these youngsters environmental deprivation tends to depress levels of functioning and self-acceptance even further. Thus, unless the family becomes involved in the counseling process and comes to accept the need to relate to and treat the retarded member more constructively, limited rehabilitation progress can be expected. Both research findings and clinical experience indicate that family relationships play a significant role in vocational rehabilitation outcomes in general, but especially in service to retarded persons.

Thus far, this discussion of counseling has dealt primarily with one-to-one relationships between a counselor and a retarded client. However, within recent years, group counseling has become increasingly accepted as another effective way of working with this group. Indeed the literature points up the need for both individual and group counseling, prescribed selectively, rather than using one or the other. One of the advantages of group counseling is that it creates a social setting that requires its retarded participants to interact acceptingly with one another. Not only do group members bring their individual problems to group sessions, but they also share and discuss these with one another, adding peer inputs to the problem-solving process. By learning that others have comparable problems, the group is drawn together, and replaces feelings of isolation and uniqueness with feelings of belongingness andd acceptance.

In a review of a large number of journal articles describing group counseling with the mentally retarded, Sternlicht (1966) suggested that the techniques used should be directive and nonverbal rather than in the verbal-insight tradition. Cotzin's (1948) description of a group he led provides an example of such an approach. In this case, the group consisted of nine institutionalized boys, mostly thirteen and fourteen years of age, with I.Q.s in the 50s and 60s, who had been troublesome and difficult to deal with in educational and other activities. At the first session the boys cursed each other, began to fight, and paid little attention to the leader. In dealing with this problem, Cotzin then organized supervised boxing matches between the boys, an activity which helped to dissipate excess energy and develop a wary respect for one another. Cotzin found that after these bouts, the group participants were able to sit quietly and listen to one another. After five or six weeks of this regimen the group had quieted down sufficiently to eliminate boxing matches from the program. At that point they still found it difficult to express their feelings toward one another and to verbalize their problems. In order to deal with this situation, Cotzin then proposed the creation of a "courtroom" with the boys taking turns as defendants and prosecutors. The prosecutor could say whatever was on his mind positively or negatively about the defendant. After the defendant had responded to what was said, the other group members, serving as a jury, added their feelings and opinions to the discussion, with Cotzin serving as the judge, keeping order and assuring everyone a chance to speak. This approach proved highly effective and throughout the sessions the boys interacted more readily and meaningfully with each other. At the end of the three-month group experience, Cotzin noted improved behavior. A one-year follow-up of the group found that seven of the nine boys had maintained or furthered their improvement, with only two regressing to earlier disturbed behavioral patterns. More than anything else, this experiment pointed up the need for creative, innovative approaches in the counseling of difficult, behaviorally disordered, and retarded clients.

Behavior modification is another fairly recently developed counseling approach that is proving effective with retarded clients. Using operant conditioning, including the concepts of reinforcement and extinction, rehabilitation counselors and other professionals are helping retarded clients to improve productivity, work behaviors, and social skills. Money, candy, tokens, and other tangible rewards are used to communicate approval to clients, thereby shaping their behavior in desired directions. Conversely, the loss of money or privileges is used to indicate dissatisfaction with, and to foster discontinuance of, undesired behavior. Other therapeutic techniques include desensitization, especially in dealing with anxiety and fear, and modeling. In the latter approach films and personal demonstrations present the desired behavior as a model to be learned, practiced, and reproduced. Behavior modification isolates specific behaviors that cause clients difficulty and enables the staff to concentrate on producing more effective behaviors. Avoiding motivational and other abstract concepts, this counseling method appears meaningful and productive, and it should be considered by counselors regardless of philosophical orientation.

Certain aspects of Adler's theory of individual psychology appear useful in counseling the mentally retarded. For example, this theory stresses the need of the disabled person to establish and strive for goals as a compensation for feelings of inferiority. Behavior change can be viewed as goal-directed activity in the context of one's lifestyle, providing a theoretical substructure for many rehabilitation procedures and phenomena. In this framework counselor attention is focused on the individual retardate's lifestyle and need satisfaction activities, rather than on some presumed attributes of the disability group as a whole. This stress on individuality is vital because behavior modification and other counseling interventions often reflect a professional's idea of what is best for a client, rather than being congruent with his individual characteristics and lifestyle. In an Adlerian context, helping persons to know what their needs are and motivating them to strive for need satisfaction may be more important than reaching specific goals, because as soon as one goal is reached it is replaced by another. In actuality, the person who continues striving tends to attain greater long-range life satisfactions.

In summary, it was noted that retarded clients should be perceived individually and differentially and as human beings who can benefit from counseling. The choice of counseling methods and techniques should be based on individual considerations and not be applied stereotypically on the basis of limited intellectual capacities. This especially applies to functional retardates whose condition may be reversible to some degree and whose potential may be close to that of the general population. Counseling this group is a challenging endeavor and requires at least as much skill and ingenuity as counseling other client populations. In contradistinction to the callous treatment retarded persons receive in our society, counseling this group requires high levels of counselor sensitivity and acceptance. The best, and not the least skilled counselors, should work with the retarded.

BIBLIOGRAPHY

Allen, R. M. and Cortazzo, A. D. *Psychosocial and Educational Aspects and Problems of Mental Retardation.* Springfield, Ill.: Charles C. Thomas, 1970.

Browning, Philip L. *Mental Retardation, Rehabilitation and Counseling.* Springfield, Ill.: Charles C. Thomas, 1974, pp. 243-247.

Chidester, Leona. "Therapeutic Results with Mentally Retarded Children," *American Journal of Orthopsychiatry,* 1934, vol. 4, pp. 464-472.

Cotzin, M. "Group Therapy with Mental Defective Problem Boys," *American Journal of Mental Deficiency,* 1948, 55: 268-283.

DeMartino, Manfred F. "Some Characteristics of the Manifest Dream Content of Mental Defectives," *Journal of Clinical Psychology,* 1954, vol. 10, pp. 175-178.

DiMichael, S. G. "Providing Full Vocational Opportunities for the Retarded Adolescents and Adults," *Journal of Rehabilitation,* 1964, 30:4, pp. 11-14.

Gardner, W. I. *Behavior Modification in Mental Retardation*. Chicago, Ill.: Aldine Publishing Co., 1971.

Heber, R. *A Manual on Terminology and Classification in Mental Retardation*. American Association On Mental Deficiency, 1961.

Krumboltz, John D. and Thoresen, Carl E. *Behavioral Counseling*. New York: Holt, Rinehart and Winston, Inc., 1969, pp. 509-515.

Rothstein, J., ed., *Mental Retardation*. New York: Holt, Rinehart and Winston, Inc., 1961.

Rusalem, H. and Cohen, M. *A Vocational Rehabilitation Day Center Program for Institutionalized Retarded Persons*. Unpublished.

Rusalem, H. and Rusalem, H. *The Learning Capacities Component in Vocational Rehabilitation*. Unpublished.

Sarason, Seymour B. "Dreams and Thematic Apperception Test Stories," *Journal of Abnormal and Social Psychology*, 1944, vol. 39, pp. 486-492.

Sternlicht, M. "Psychotherapeutic Procedures With the Retarded," in Ellis, N. *International Review of Research in Mental Retardation*. New York: Academic Press, 1966, vol. 2, pp. 279-354.

Thorne, Frederick T. "Counseling and Psychotherapy with Mental Defectives," *American Journal of Mental Deficiency*, 1948, vol. 52, pp. 263-271.

Walsh, W. S. "Dreams of the Feeble Minded," *Medical Records*, 1920, vol. 97, pp. 395-398.

IMPLICATIONS FOR REHABILITATION PRACTICE

While there may be important legal and administrative reasons for defining retardation in orthodox I.Q. terms, such definitions and labels can become more of a barrier than a facilitator in the rehabilitation of the mentally retarded. What counselors need is not a more exact diagnostic category, but more definitive data concerning actual client functioning. What a client can or cannot learn to do is more revealing for rehabilitation purposes than test scores, school grades, or subgroupings. A multifaceted evaluation utilizing all available techniques and services should be used to identify client strengths and potentialities.

Just as the elimination of architectural barriers changes the status of some homebound clients, so can the restructuring of the environment enable some retardates to function on virtually a nonretardate level in some activities. Individualization of services and careful selection of occupational objectives based on client characteristics and capabilities is the optimum way to maximize rehabilitation effectiveness with the mentally retarded.

Despite the existence of a substantial body of research and clinical reports indicating that retardates can and do benefit from counseling, considerable bias against the use of this service with them still persists. Traditionally, the limited counseling available to the retarded has been of a superficial nature, reflecting an attitude that these clients cannot really be helped through this medium to function adequately in face-to-face relationships. This may be true in some situations, but for higher level retardates it often is a mistaken and inequitable conclusion.

Retarded clients sometimes present problems in relating to others, in evolving a realistic self-concept, and in satisfying needs in a social manner, just as do others who come for counseling. Both individual and group counseling techniques have their place in the rehabilitation process. Furthermore, since families play a vital role in the development of retardate persons, counselors must involve them in any problem-solving process. Counseling retarded individuals is a difficult and challenging undertaking that requires the intervention of the most and not the least skilled and experienced of practitioners. Today, American rehabilitation is committed to nothing less.

CHAPTER X

ECOLOGICAL APPROACHES TO COUNSELING THE PHYSICALLY DISABLED

SETTING THE SCENE

The "physically disabled" comprise such a vast number of individuals, types of disabilities, and varying life styles as to render the term almost meaningless. As Rusalem indicates in this chapter, there are large numbers of physically disabled who are functionally capable and for whom counseling is much like that practiced with the nondisabled. On the other hand, there is a significant group of severely disabled individuals whose problems are many and difficult, and who, for a variety of reasons, cannot benefit from the traditional type of counseling normally practiced by rehabilitation counselors. These clients are beset by environmental and situational handicaps, in addition to the usual psychosocial problems that lend themselves to face to face contacts, and require that counselors look beyond their usual practices if these handicaps are to be surmounted.

One of the difficulties involved in developing innovative approaches to working with the severely disabled is that this cannot be taught to student counselors in the same way as are various counseling theories. Innovation flows from one's creativity and is usually a response to unique situations requiring unique solutions. While much knowledge can be transmitted from teacher to student, no one has yet determined how to teach creativity, or how to use it in innovational activities.

This should be borne in mind when reviewing Rusalem's chapter. He selected five environmental and situational problems that, in his experience, have not been dealt with adequately in the past, and then suggested counselor interventions that might resolve or alleviate them. This is not to say that there aren't other problem areas of similar importance, or that there might not be more effective approaches to their resolution. In selecting these problems and offering his way of coping with them, Rusalem was seeking a way of stimulating the creative potential of his readers. He is alerting all of us in the field of rehabilitation that we cannot rest on our laurels, or blind ourselves to the fact that there exists a large clientele of severely disabled individuals who have largely been neglected in the past because they present so great a challenge to our creativity.

CHAPTER X

ECOLOGICAL APPROACHES TO COUNSELING THE PHYSICALLY DISABLED

Herbert Rusalem

Residual physical disability introduces highly significant problems into the lives of the ill and injured. These problems have been explored extensively by behavioral and medical scientists, virtually all of whom confirm the everyday observation that the consequences of physical disability tend to generate heightened needs for counseling. Obviously, these needs differ in detail from individual to individual depending on the person's life history, current disability, social-psychological situation, personality organization, physical symptoms, and interpersonal ecology. Since the consequences of disability vary widely, counselors of the physically disabled need to be responsive to the individuality of the client, avoiding stereotypes and unwarranted categorization. Attempts to associate various physical disabilities with recurring concomitant specific psychological responses have not been successful. In essence, the physically limited have been found to be as individual in their reactions to their conditions as all people are to any other class of unfortunate events. The incidence and range of any response class (such as withdrawal) is about the same for the physically disabled as for any other group in society.

In this context, it may seem superfluous to devote a chapter in this book to counseling procedures for physically limited persons since, as suggested above, they are so much like other counselees. To a certain extent, this conclusion is warranted. Indeed, this chapter could well terminate at this point and, without further orientation, many readers of this volume could fulfill their professional face-to-face counseling responsibilities to physically handicapped clients fairly effectively without further specialized knowledge or skill.

In actuality, the psychosocial damage imposed upon the members of this client group is not significantly different from that observed in physically unimpaired individuals who suffer the loss of a loved one, endure continuing environmental deprivation, suffer prolonged isolation from others, or encounter extended loss of affection, approval, or appreciation. General counseling techniques that are used to deal with these common nondisability life problems apply equally well to the physically limited. Apparently, then, no new special counseling school, approach, or procedure is required to work with them. Therefore, as in the field of education, most physically disabled counselees can be "mainstreamed" (that is, helped by counselors who are equipped to serve people, in general) in a variety of settings. In view of this, we will avoid a detailed discussion of face-to-face counseling techniques that are relevant to this group. Such techniques may best be explored by consulting "general" counseling texts and by taking "general" counseling courses.

Having noted this, however, it should be indicated that if one looks beyond "orthodox" face-to-face counseling, there is something special about working with the physically limited. For this reason, the remainder of this chapter will be placed in the framework of a form of counseling that extends beyond the process through which two people talk together over a period of time so that one (the counselee) can resolve some of his life problems in a therapeutic relationship with another (the counselor). In addition to face-to-face client contacts, this broader view of counseling assigns responsibility to the counselor for assessing and altering unfavorable aspects of a disabled individual's physical and social environment in the belief that an unfavorable environment constitutes an important core of many rehabilitation-related problems.

This formulation acknowledges that the onset of a serious physical condition often renders an individual vulnerable to numerous life problems, some of which can be helped substantially by talking them through with a professional worker. However, many other problems are situational and, if dealt with properly in environmental terms, are short-term in nature. In brief, face-to-face counseling is highly useful in helping the disabled person over some of the rapids of the disability experiences and in reshaping certain responses to altered physical and social status. Yet, some of the most persistent adaptation problems of physically disabled persons are not rooted within themselves but are imposed upon them by an insensitive and rigid social structure that denies them essential human rights. All too often, extended face-to-face counseling is provided to basically intact physically handicapped individuals in an effort to strengthen them to cope with an unreasonable society. However useful this approach may be, it does little to alter that unreasonable society and, whether they are strengthened or not, the counselees are compelled to go on, day after day and year after year, coping with apparently immovable obstacles erected in their path by the world in which they reside. Under these circumstances, continuing face-to-face counseling is comparable to blaming the victim. Rather than dealing with the exploiter, we treat the exploited.

An ecological approach to physical disability holds to the view that most adventitiously physically limited persons were emotionally intact, though not necessarily models of good mental health, prior to the acquisition of their disabilities. When the disability appears, these relatively intact individuals do not automatically undergo substantial long-range psychic changes. On the contrary, they continue to be the people they were, responding in characteristic fashion to the new crises that have been generated in their lives by the onset of disability. The available evidence does not support suppositions of a marked long-range diminution of adjustive capacity or coping resources. When personality disorders do occur among the physically disabled, they are not necessarily a direct simplistic consequence of the illness, accident, or injury that incapacitates them. On the contrary, these long-range effects most often are a function of the preexisting personality and the psychological and social field in which the physically limited client plays out his role as a disabled person. This role often is so depersonalizing and demeaning that it, more than anything else, taxes the individuals' psychic resources and renders them vulnerable to mental health problems.

As rehabilitation ecologists see the counseling process with the physically limited, the central purpose of counseling with this group is not universally the alleviation of mental health-related problems, however important these may be in individual cases. Much more compelling is the prevention and early arrest of such emotional problems by focusing counseling skill and energy as fully as possible on the social components of physical disability which render the disability experience far more dangerous than do the physical symptoms. Face-to-face counseling is useful in general and especially so in relation to early emotional reactions to physical disability and in situations in which long-term psychosocial deprivation and neglect (such as in the homebound) have generated serious and continuing mental health and adjustment problems. Accepting this does not weaken the belief that physical limitations are not the physically disabled person's worst enemy; on the contrary, it is the society in which he lives.

Although a broad spectrum of social and environmental influences could be cited in support of this position, for the sake of brevity only five of them will be discussed below:

(1) *The Physical Properties of the Environment.* Architectural barriers constitute the single most frustrating environmental limitation in the life of the physically disabled person. Environmental obstacles of one kind or another continue to restrict participation in education, employment, rehabilitation, and social interaction by hundreds of thousands of severely disabled persons. For example, regardless of the face-to-face counseling received, homebound persons remain homebound unless and until the physical barriers that confront them are removed or unless they are transferred to a barrier-free environment. Unfortunately, architectural barriers abound in most communities, effectively reducing physically limited persons' ability to enter public and private buildings, use sanitary facilities, enjoy drama, theater, and art, borrow books from the library, enjoy a favorite restaurant, attend sports events, travel about the community, and leave their residences for whatever purpose whenever they wish. Isolated from essential employment, educational, and social activities by these unreasonable physical barriers, severely disabled persons understandably develop anger, frustration, and disappointment that, despite face-to-face counseling, tends to persist as long as their legitimate needs are thwarted by unnecessary and remediable artificial barriers.

(2) *Experience Deprivation.* Physical disability tends to limit persons' ability to reach out to the environment. For example, many disabled people cannot readily move about the community, enter freely into community activities, or, in some cases, even leave their homes or neighborhoods on personal missions. Thus,

their potential range of life experiences frequently is sharply diminished and, in time, exposes the persons to the long-range deleterious effects of experience deprivation. Among these effects are reduced alertness, decrements in intellectual and cognitive competency, social disengagement, excessive passivity and hopelessness, depression, and overconcern with the self. Concomitantly, as the duration of a physical disability lengthens into years, previous community and social relationships tend to become less meaningful and are not readily replaced by others. Consequently, friends visit less frequently, neighbors intervene less regularly, and social agencies gradually become less vigorous in their attempts to deliver needed home and neighborhood-based services. These hazards of experience deprivation are often so consequential that their handicapping influence can become more limiting than the original physical disability.

(3) *Exclusionary Attitudes.* Closed minds in the community can be as effective as functional limitations in excluding the physically disabled person from employment, education, recreation, and interpersonal relationships. A wealth of social-psychological research confirms the existence in American society of widespread negative, avoidant, and exclusionary public attitudes toward various subgroups of disabled persons. These attitude systems have their roots firmly established in tradition, history, custom, and parental teaching, but whatever their source, they constitute a continuing irrational source of deprivation to the physically disabled group, complicating their adaptations and exacerbating their functional limitations. Because of these negative attitudes, clients' life-space and aspirations often become unnecessarily constricted in all areas of living. Although attempts are made to modify attitudes and to support disabled persons in coping with them, such attitudes usually continue to thwart handicapped persons, regardless of the face-to-face counseling made available to them.

(4) *Neglect of Learning Problems.* Persons who acquire their physical limitations in the adolescent and adult years almost always are required to learn new survival skills at a stage in life when the mastery of radically different responses normally comes with difficulty. Learning to walk, talk, use their hands, see, hear, and

behave in ways that differ from their earlier life experiences makes heavy demands on established response systems that often are resistant to change. Consequently, the learning demands required in mastering new devices, tools, ideas, attitudes, behaviors, and approaches constantly challenge the physically disabled client. Indeed, counseling itself requires extensive learning in terms of understanding, accepting, and incorporating into themselves new and more functional views of their capacities, relationship to the world, and use of themselves in attaining life goals. Despite the crucial nature of learning in rehabilitation, most rehabilitation programs function as though learning problems do not exist. Thus, few rehabilitation workers are aware of the learning capacities of their clients, the learning demands of the rehabilitation environment, and the techniques of bringing learning capacities and task demands into balance with each other. As a consequence, relatively few physically disabled clients are instructed through appropriate teaching procedures in evaluation, counseling, training, and employment.

(5) *Ineffective Service Delivery.* The rehabilitation services offered to physically handicapped persons vary widely in effectiveness. All too many of these services are fragmentary rather than comprehensive, staffed by stereotyping rather than creative personnel, "hit-and-run" rather than long-term, employment focused rather than life-oriented, spottily available to those who cannot leave their homes or neighborhoods, rather than universal, and not infrequently insensitive to what it means to be physically disabled in a world designed for the nonhandicapped. Even highly professional workers tend to look the other way in instances of service ineffectiveness in their communities because they are integral parts of that very system. As a consequence, they mute their criticisms and make few waves. In any event, thousands of physically disabled persons who could be helped through a more effective delivery of existing rehabilitation resources continue to fail because the systems and the personnel running them are inadequate. The current practice of counseling the client to accept the "realities" of faulty service delivery provides cold comfort when individual need for adequate rehabilitation assistance is so great.

Given these five problem areas, little wonder then, that the thoughtful physically handicapped rehabilitation clients are perplexed by some of the things that go on in rehabilitation. For example, as emotionally intact persons, they may continue to be confronted by problems of architectural barriers, experience deprivation, exclusionary attitudes, neglect of their learning problems, and ineffective services. Despite the environmental basis of their difficulties, the only answer that may be offered to them is talking about these problems. As clients see it, "accepting" and "working" with these situations makes little sense when, in reality, something should be done about the external conditions that baffle them. Understandably, they come to feel at times that they are being held responsible for what society is doing to them and that rehabilitation workers are preoccupied with pinpointing their deficiencies rather than those of the community. In these cases, the counselor is deluded by their psychotherapeutic ideology since the difficulties are in the environment, not in the client. Indeed, as one works with physically handicapped persons one is impressed with how intact they really are and how well they are coping with a most difficult disability experience. Extensive therapeutically oriented help is rarely needed in this area; on the contrary, the need is for conversion of unfavorable environments into more favorable ones through specialized counseling procedures.

Each of the five areas of environmental thwarting for the physically disabled noted above suggests one or more preferred counseling interventions which transcend the usual face-to-face talking-through counseling approaches. These interventions are described briefly below in the context of the environmental limitations with which they are most closely associated.

(1) *Counseling in the Architectural Barriers Area.* For the most part, rehabilitation workers counsel physically disabled persons rather than those who limit and deprive them. To counter those who deny their human rights, physically handicapped people need service personnel who can operate as legislative expediters, enforcers of human rights provisions, community and educational advocates, and watchdogs of human decency rather than therapists. In this framework, counselors will help in expediting the enactment of legislation that reduce or eliminate architectural barriers, the enforcement of administrative provisions

that implement favorable court decisions and enactments, and the protection of the free access of physically disabled persons to facilities, services, and programs open to everyone in the community. Some of this ecological counseling may be in conjunction with the orthodox face-to-face counseling modes, but most of it will follow the change agent advocacy model.

(2)   *Counseling in the Experience Deprivation Area.* The central approach in this area is an aggressive family counseling service that orients and trains family groups to provide heightened stimulation to severely handicapped persons in conjunction with concurrent efforts made to open wider the doors of community schools, colleges, community centers, fraternal organizations, churches, synagogues, and other service centers. Family members should receive preparation not only for their immediate role as deliverers of environmental stimulation but as sources of pressure to be applied to the community that can influence a larger number of facilities to admit and serve physically handicapped persons more meaningfully than in the past. In addition, rehabilitation workers will be required to counsel the media to offer educational and social programs and materials that offset the isolation and disengagement that threaten many physicaly handicapped people. Simultaneously, rehabilitation workers function as community organizers who form volunteer, student, and paraprofessional groups that interact more fully with the physically disabled person, and as developers of networks of coordinated client stimulation services that can be brought to the severely physically limited persons when they are unable to reach out to them.

(3)   *Counseling in Relation to Exclusionary Attitudes.* Rehabilitation workers serving the physically disabled should be nondisabled individuals and groups in the community who concern themselves with the destructive effects and undemocratic nature of exclusionary attitudes. In view of the fact that some attitudes toward physical atypicality change slowly and painfully and that attitude change procedures sometimes require extended periods of time to be effective, interventions that have both immediate and long-term payoff should be conducted concurrently. Thus, while efforts to reshape enduring attitudes go forward, rehabilitation workers should support the activities of

groups of disabled persons committed to the protection and extension of the human rights of the handicapped. Through aggressive advocacy and, if necessary, direct social action such as demonstrations, picketing, and the use of political power, rehabilitation workers should foster public behaviors which, regardless of persistent underlying attitudes, assure physically handicapped persons their essential dignity and human rights. This is done in the belief that attitudes that cannot be changed by counseling may have to be endured by a disabled person, but never should public behaviors be permitted that violate human rights and human decency. Through vigilant monitoring of the manner in which the community treats its disabled citizens and through maximizing the opportunities that are afforded them to effectuate change, rehabilitation workers should perform the essential counseling function of shaping the behavior of community gatekeepers who often determine the fate of disabled individuals.

(4) *Counseling in Countering the Neglect of Learning Problems.* Most rehabilitation counselors are trained to recognize and modify mental health deterrents to rehabilitation success. Deriving status and satisfaction from their psychotherapeutic counseling role, these workers are sensitive to emotional and adjustment factors in the rehabilitation process. Unfortunately, this is not all there is to rehabilitation. Indeed, learning difficulties often are a major source of rehabilitation failure and underachievement among physically disabled clients. Techniques pioneered by Rusalem and Rusalem in the Learning Capacities Research Project enable counselors of the physically limited to initiate "first aid" learning capacities evaluation techniques to ascertain the sites of learning problems in a gross way and, then, in conjunction with learning capacities specialists, evaluators, trainers, and placement counselors, to design instructional interventions (including counseling) that are compatible with the client's learning attributes. In this context, every rehabilitation worker is, among other things, a learning capacities service provider, making certain that the client's learning style is as carefully considered in formulating and implementing a rehabilitation plan as are mental health considerations.

(5) *Ineffective Services.* It is universally acknowledged that physically

disabled clients should have access to all available community services for which they qualify. However, in view of the deficiencies that exist in such services, interest is shifting from an acceptance of existing services to the counselor's growing role in reshaping community programs. In the course of this shift, counselors are moving on from being mere coordinators of clients' programs to functioning as activist advocates of more effective client assistance, whether it be through modifying inadequate existing rehabilitation services or taking the initiative to create needed new services. For example, in serving as a community organizer, the counselor of the physically disabled should aggressively attack architectural barriers imbedded in construction plans for new buildings, question the legality and fairness of arbitrary exclusions that relegate physically limited clients to secondary positions, challenge service providers who are insensitive to client needs and rights, and expose local and state rehabilitation processes that feature mass approaches and occupational stereotypes in contradistinction to the high level of individualization that should prevail in this field.

The proper implementation of counseling in the five areas noted above calls for a new breed of counselors, who are not tied by a professional umbilical cord to their offices where they dispense therapeutically oriented service to physically disabled clients. Instead, in accordance with the belief that most physically disabled clients are capable of running their own lives, making their own decisions, and coping independently with reasonable obstacles, such counselors should function where the action is—in the crucible of the community where the real deterrents to rehabilitation lie. Although face-to-face client counseling continues to be a viable intervention in these cases, it does not dominate the rehabilitation process, but supports and strengthens the central effort to reshape the environment.

Rehabilitation counselors who have been trained in, and have made a professional commitment to, the talking-through mode may not always find it easy to revise their procedures to fit this concept. Furthermore, it may well be that other classes of clients require greater infusions of psychotherapeutically oriented counseling interventions but even this is open to question. Whatever the case may be, counselors should recognize that physical disability generates problems that lie not so much within the psyche of disabled persons as in the human and physical ecology in which they function. However worthwhile they may be, attempts to treat internal emotional variables have little impact upon a deterrent external environment which, despite the personal gains made by clients in face-to-face counseling, continues to deprive them of adequate opportunities and resources. Although physically limited clients and their families can, in some cases, be trained to become their own best advocates, we cannot expect them, as individuals, to have extensive success in their efforts to reorient society. In most instances, if environmental change is to be engineered on behalf of the physically limited, it will have to flow from the activities of counselors, individually and in groups. With counselors applying their counseling skills to a denying society, they will target their efforts more directly to the real crux of the problem.

This newer and more appropriate counseling role vis-à-vis the physically disabled client group promises to yield more realistic and enduring rehabilitation case closures. All too often, persisting in face-to-face counseling as the dominant rehabilitation treatment is more beneficial for counselors than for clients. Indeed, physically disabled clients more often than their counselors clearly and correctly perceive their problems in environmental rather than mental health terms. Since the restrictive community usually does not change spontaneously to provide equity to the physically disabled, the current situation has a self-reinforcing quality. For substantial change to occur, social cognitive dissonance needs to be created through a form of counseling that has such components as confrontation, pressure, and legal action. Rehabilitation counseling for the physically limited client cannot continue addressing itself to the wrong problem. The aggressor is society; the victim is the physically disabled person. Treating the victim is only one aspect of the situation and a secondary one at that. The main treatment arena is the community and the family.

IMPLICATIONS FOR REHABILITATION PRACTICE

The essence of Rusalem's argument is that there are problems whose solution lies beyond the capabilities of the client. As he points out, a homebound individual might be emotionally intact, intellectually talented and socially willing and yet be helpless in overcoming architectural barriers, experimental deprivation, learning problems, the exclusionary attitudes of others, and ineffective services offered by rehabilitation workers. In a large part these problems are rooted in society, and their solutions can only be achieved by an enlightened citizenry that desires change, What is needed are counselors who, in addition to possessing counseling know-how and skills, also possess a social awareness that will motivate them to undertake advocacy roles.

The fact that so many counselors desire to function like psychotherapists implies that university training programs may be fostering such an orientation. In many institutions, counseling courses and clinical experiences that focus on individual dynamics make up the heart of a rehabilitation counseling curriculum, with relatively few occasions occurring when social issues are discussed. Thus, this area may be somewhat unexplored in some training programs. If the current emphasis on dealing with the severely disabled is to be more than just a passing fad, university educators and field supervisors will have to consider how their current training programs might be changed to heighten student awareness of society's role in creating and exacerbating handicaps.

Social and rehabilitation agencies, both voluntary and public, have also contributed to inhibiting counselor advocacy roles. Most agencies are fearful of creating an image of being controversial, or appearing political, and consequently discourage professionals from campaigning for legislative change. Since so much of rehabilitation is conducted in the governmental arena, requiring interagency goodwill and cooperation, agencies often feel they have to adopt a neutral position, lest some political leadership be offended by questioning established policies toward disabled individuals.

In order for counselors to develop innovative practices with the severely disabled, practices that extend far beyond the counselor's office or the client's home, universities and agency executives will have to commit themselves to supporting their professional staff efforts to bring about social change. Creativity, like plants, can only flourish in an atmosphere of "tender-loving-care" watered by supportive actions.

CHAPTER XI

THE JOB PLACEMENT PROCESS

SETTING THE SCENE

The central characteristic of vocational rehabilitation is that whatever service route the counselor and the client takes, the objective is remunerative employment. Such an objective is clear, unequivocal, and inescapable. For the vocational rehabilitation process to be considered successful for any individual, the end product must be an appropriate and satisfying job. Unlike other forms of human service that pursue less tangible outcomes (such as an improved sense of self-worth, greater life satisfaction, or enhanced mental health), vocational rehabilitation imposes upon its practitioners a sharply defined accountability. Although other social and psychosocial benefits may accrue to the client, the central criterion of success is suitable employment.

From 1920 to about 1955, rehabilitation workers did not have to be reminded of their vocational mission. In those days, many counselors were recruited from industry or public employment service offices and they brought with them a keen sense of the vocational rehabilitation and employment objective. In the mid-1950s, it became obvious that job placement alone was just a single component in a complex treatment process and that rehabilitation counselors had to be trained in a variety of psychosocial skills as well. Thus, new master's level rehabilitation counselors began to flow out of graduate schools with specialties in psychology, special education, and other behavioral science departments. From the earlier extreme focus upon vocational factors, the field moved to the other extreme which emphasized psychosocial factors. In the process vocational placement got lost somewhere along the line.

Today's broadened view of vocational rehabilitation accommodates the newer behavioral science perspective but, simultaneously, recognizes the key role of the employment objective. Consequently, the developmental pendulum is gradually swinging back toward a middle position with vocational placement being accorded a more prominent place in the rehabilitation service spectrum. As this occurs, rehabilitation workers are developing a need for more sophisticated placement techniques, both to better understand the vocational problems and potentials of their clients and, where required, to effectuate selective placements on their own. The chapter that follows presents the distilled wisdom of a specialist who continued to advocate placement even when it was not fashionable to do so and who now sets forth "hard-nosed" practical placement suggestions that are rarely found in the current literature.

CHAPTER XI

THE JOB PLACEMENT PROCESS

Daniel Sinick

"Without Placement, There Is No Rehabilitation" was the theme of a conference held in late 1973. This emphasis is needed to counteract the notion of some counselors that they "have rehabilitated John Doe and now he just has to be placed." Vocational rehabilitation is not accomplished until the client has become a satisfactory and satisfied employee in a suitable occupation.

It is true that rehabilitative services toward nonvocational goals might benefit clients whose potentials or values are not consonant with employment, but most clients would like to work and are capable of working. The general aim of vocational rehabilitation is therefore almost universally applicable.

Counselors apparently have other reasons for deemphasizing job placement. Survey responses from 72 of 87 state vocational rehabilitation agencies (Ninth Institute on Rehabilitation Services, 1972) gave as a top priority problem encountered regarding placement—after "current job market" and "employer resistance"—"counselors' resistance to placement" (p. 25). Why are counselors resistant to placement? "What ever happened to job placement?" is a similar question asked by Flannagan (1974).

Placement is seen by some as too mundane for their professional attention, which they prefer to focus on the psychodynamics of the client's private world. Placement is seemingly below their dignity. In reality, placement calls for high level professional skills, including understanding of the employer's psychodynamics and sensitivity to numerous nuances of employer verbal and nonverbal communications. Reluctant employers are just as challenging as reluctant (and compliant) clients.

The insecurity often underlying the below-professional-dignity stance is paralleled by insecurity based upon erroneous or exaggerated perceptions of placement or upon lack of placement expertise. Counselors may believe that automation has eliminated all blue-collar jobs, that intelligence is directly related to job performance, that clients must be overqualified to obtain jobs. Counselors thus use straw men to support their lack of motivation for placement.

As to lack of placement expertise, counselors are like clients in dreading rejection by employers. Such dread is natural and understandable, especially if counselors are unfamiliar with strategies and techniques that can minimize employer rejection. A major purpose of this chapter is to make counselors better informed about employers, placement strategies, and placement counseling.

A final antiplacement posture of counselors that must be countered is that they need not know about placement if other people are doing it. Some rehabilitation settings have their own placement specialists or rely upon the State Employment Service for placement. Counselors need to know about testing and other evaluative methods, however, whether they or others perform the actual procedures. By knowing as much as they can about placement procedures, counselors will be better able to carry out their *responsibility* for placement of their clients and to do a more informed job of vocational rehabilitation counseling.

Counseling Toward Placement

Even where others perform the function of placement, therefore, counselor responsibility to see that their clients are placed necessitates counseling not only toward vocational plans but also toward placement. Relinquishment of this professional responsibility results in the languishing of disproportionate numbers of clients in the limbo often called "ready for employment." That label or one like it means simply that a vocational plan has been written; readiness for employment may require counseling geared to that goal.

Such counseling is an appropriate part of the counseling toward vocational plans and their implementation, but when not integrated into preplan counseling it needs to be provided afterward. The need to do so with rehabilitation clients is made clear by the demonstrated need to do so with college students and graduates (Stevens and Schneider, 1967). These authors emphasized the importance of "placement readiness"; Way and Lipton (1973) similarly emphasized "employment readiness."

If counseling toward placement is to be effective, clients' readiness for placement may first have to be ascertained and, when inadequate, improved. Stevens and Schneider (1971) described various personality characteristics associated with high, moderate, and low placement readiness. College seniors high in readiness tended to be less submissive and dependent and more tough-minded and emotionally stable.

Complex psychodynamic variables, together with simple earthy ones, complicate the counseling of rehabilitation clients toward placement. Clients are excessively dependent, inappropriately independent, and sometimes both simultaneously. They may overemphasize or underemphasize a disability. They may exhibit extreme anxiety or insufficient anxiety—until the approach of a job interview touches the panic button.

Competent counseling can unravel complexities by dealing with them in relation to realities like job interviews and other aspects of the job hunt. Psychotherapy is not required to prepare clients for placement. Sheppard and Belitsky (1968, p. 14) consider it "feasible to modify the jobseeking behavior of many persons through intensive instruction, counseling, or reorientation. . . ."

Clients may need readying for such tasks as developing and pursuing job leads, writing letters of application and completing application blanks, preparing résumés and portfolios of their work, taking employment tests, and organizing information about themselves and prospective employers. Information about an employer and about the job sought can strengthen a client both cognitively and affectively in the job interview.

In addition to individual counseling, group counseling is applicable to the development of rehabilitation clients' jobseeking skills (Frank, 1968), as is group instruction (McClure, 1972). The group process often reduces extreme anxiety, induces motivation for placement, and displaces diffidence with realistic self-confidence, equipping clients with know-how for navigating the shoals of jobseeking.

Although placement counseling techniques and tools have been presented elsewhere (*Job Seeking Skills Reference Manual, 1971;* Sinick,

1970, Chapter 5), attention is focused here on a problem specific to many rehabilitation clients—"To tell or not to tell?" Job applications still ask about nervous breakdowns, convulsive seizures, alcoholism, criminal records, and other matters historic, controlled, or in remission. Clients need help in deciding about disclosure of an invisible disability or about lifting the lid off what is past.

The key concept is: Counselors provide needed assistance but clients make their own decisions. Factors affecting client decisions and entering into counseling discussions may include the stability of the condition, its overt or covert nature, the prospective job content and context, and attitudes of the client and others toward the condition and toward telling about it. Counselor attitudes such as "Honesty is the best policy" do not yield the best practice for individual clients. Pertinent issues and information are discussed by Olshansky, Grob, and Ekdahl (1972) in regard to ex-mental patients and by Sinick (1974) in regard to persons with epilepsy.

Job Placement Strategies

Clients prepared for placement are potentially active participants —partners, indeed—in the jobseeking process. For jobseeking to turn into *jobfinding*, broad strategies must be mapped and tactical techniques applied. Since strategies and tactics are difficult to differentiate, the broader term is used here to embrace both approaches.

The client as a partner who assumes important placement responsibilities was emphasized by Salomone (1971). Self-placement is a highly desirable outcome, for several reasons. Self-esteem and a sense of independence are enhanced. Clients who obtain their own jobs tend to stay in them longer. When job changes are necessary, however, clients have gained some capability for placing themselves.

To avoid possible confusion, self-employment is to be distinguished from self-placement, although the two may go hand-in-hand. Some clients experience such difficulty in being employed by others that the only recourse may be self-employment. "Being your own boss" is also a dominant drive in some clients. Despite the risks, running one's own business is a strategic goal not to be ignored.

A basic strategy is to serve employers as well as clients. Qualified applicants are offered to meet employer needs, with no attempt to unload unlikely prospects upon unsuspecting employers. While qualifications are stressed in employer contacts, relevant limitations are not concealed, though presented positively. Counselors who are knowledgeable about employer needs and "show that they care" have been called upon as resources or consultants.

Employers can be helped with the induction and orientation of new employees and the adoption of simple job modifications. The latter are generally appreciated as beneficial for other employees and for the overall operation. Employers can also be helped to appreciate, especially in tight labor markets, the unrealistic nature of arbitrary medical and educational requirements. They can be apprised, too, of the availability of follow-up services for any adjustments on the job.

Follow-up services are part of placement services, ensuring employer satisfaction with work performance and client satisfaction with the job. Perhaps better called "postplacement services," such assistance is different from statistical studies of program effectiveness and may precede as well as follow case closure (Ninth Institute on Rehabilitation Services, 1972, pp. 83-84). The purposes and procedures of postplacement services have been delineated elsewhere (Sinick, 1970, pp. 64-69).

Employers as collaborators is another strategy that benefits both sides—or places employers and counselors on the same side. Called upon for their expertise, employers have provided suggestions and referrals for hard-to-place clients and have even hired some themselves. Committees of employers have assisted various communities in improving clients' jobseeking skills and effectuating employment (Zuger, 1971).

Whether through collaboration or otherwise, it is sound strategy to reduce employers' unfamiliarity with rehabilitation clients and client potentials. In this case, familiarity does not breed contempt. Demonstrations of actual work performance are best, in employers' work settings or in rehabilitation workshops, but samples of clients' work can be impressive, too. Seeing what clients can do could lessen the need for "education" of employers toward change of negative attitudes.

Clients and counselors must be prepared, nonetheless, for the numerous objections raised by employers regarding possible accidents, absenteeism, turnover, and other sources of increased costs (*Manual on Selective Placement of the Disabled*, 1965). In view of the profit-making motivation of most employers, shared concern for productivity and costs is a better strategy than appeals to their sense of social responsibility. Better, too, than unsolicited citations of studies comparing disabled and nondisabled workers (Sinick, 1968) are letters from satisfied employers, who not uncommonly request "more like the last one."

A caution is in order here: "Better" is a relative term that does not mean termination of competing strategies. The strategy of strategies is to use whatever works. And different strategies work with different counselors, clients, and employers.

A case in point is the question as to whether large or small employers are better prospects for job placement. Small firms are sometimes regarded as more personal and humanitarian, with greater social responsibility, and are less likely to use probing application blanks. Yet numerous clients have been placed with large organizations, some of which have special policies for hiring disabled workers. Not to be disregarded is clients' preferences as to size of employer enterprises.

The largest employer in the United States, the federal government, accepts certification by state vocational rehabilitation or Veterans Administration counselors that a client is qualified for a particular job; the usual competitive procedures are waived. Disabled applicants who meet minimum qualifications may be appointed for a trial period before being made permanent. When tests must be taken, special provisions apply to such groups as the blind, the deaf, and the cerebral palsied. Some of these favorable federal procedures (U.S. Civil Service Commission, 1972) are also practised by a number of states.

Community resources of all kinds can be enlisted in the service of job placement. Large and small employers are members of business and trade associations, chambers of commerce, and other organizations that fit broad strategies. The author (1968) has suggested coordination of rehabilitation placement efforts with public and private employment agencies—to reduce duplication (and annoyance to employers) —and creation of a client-oriented clearing house of job opportunities.

Information About Employers

The value of employer information has been mentioned in relation to client confidence and competence in job interviews and counselor effectiveness in serving employers as well as clients. Such information relates pervasively to the development of appropriate job opportunities and to successful placements, "successful" meaning placements that are suitable and satisfying to clients and satisfactory to employers.

Pertinent information includes numerous facets of the employer's enterprise: its general nature, its physical and psychosocial characteristics, its work force, factors affecting work and worker, and personnel practices. Since this wealth (or welter) of information cannot be covered within the confines of this chapter, selected items are presented together with some possible implications for placement.

The nature of the employer's enterprise might embrace straightforward information like whether services are provided or goods are manufactured, distributed, or sold. Some clients' values concern these distinctions and whether the enterprise is for profit or not for profit. Subtler information involves variables like organizational climate: Is it heavily authoritarian or reasonably humanitarian? The sensitive need satisfactions of rehabilitation clients are not to be written off on the basis of presumed desperation for a job.

Physical characteristics encompass accessibility to public or private transportation; accessibility of work place, eating place, and rest room; and such environmental variables as temperature, noise, and vibration. Any of these factors might bar placement of particular clients, unless adjustments can be made; for example, simple ramps can sometimes be installed for wheelchairs.

Psychosocial factors include employee characteristics and interpersonal relations. The age range, sex, and minority representation of employees may be of importance to clients, as well as opportunity for conversation. Is supervision supportive, punitive, or simply insufficient?

Besides the work force's composition, employee skill levels may relate to client confidence and comfort. More mundane aspects of the work force involve employee turnover and current and expected job openings. Job prospects in the near future can be overlooked when employers are asked only about vacancies at the time of contact.

Additional factors affecting work and worker are work hours and work shifts, hourly vs. piecework pay, rotation of work tasks, work hazards, fringe benefits, busy and slack seasons, lines of promotion and transfer, and prospect for continued employment. Whether pay is on an hourly or piecework basis could spell success or failure for an employee. Work shifts could constitute a negative factor or an opportunity for clients who require special schedules.

Personnel practices relate to recruitment, hiring, firing, and rehiring.

How employees are sought and who is responsible for hiring are essential pieces of information, as are such requirements as education, experience, union membership, tools, medical examination, employment tests, and—despite equal opportunity legislation—sex and age. Recruitment methods may afford counselors a collaborative role. Particular requirements serve as guideposts (or red, green, or caution lights) for placement counseling.

On-the-job training is a possible personnel practice counselors must be familiar with, as it is an opening wedge for clients who might otherwise not be hired. Although its format varies widely, it generally provides part of the trainee-employee's pay, usually in a diminishing ratio to the employer's contribution. OJT thus offers workers at reduced initial cost to employers, who can observe rehabilitation clients demonstrate their competence.

OJT has been a practice supported not only by vocational rehabilitation agencies but also by the National Alliance of Businessmen, the U.S. Department of Labor, and the U.S. Department of Health, Education, and Welfare. Special OJT projects have been conducted by the National Association for Retarded Children and the International Association of Rehabilitation Facilities, which has published a useful *On-Job-Training Program Procedures Manual* (1974). A variation on the theme of wage subsidization has been described by Knape (1972).

Acquiring Employer Information

Counselors have countless sources of the kinds of information sketched in the preceding section. In counseling, placing, and providing post-placement services, counselors learn a good deal about employers and job opportunities. In reading newspapers, alert counselors notice relevant information and possible leads in both help wanted and business advertisements, in items about new business and new construction, and in items about job changes, promotions, and even obituaries. Similar information is found in some magazines and trade journals. Telephone directories and directories of manufacturers and distributors are added sources.

Among organizations that might serve as sources are trade and professional associations, chambers of commerce, civic and service clubs, voluntary agencies, unions, and political parties. Available in some communities are associations of personnel directors, training directors, or safety engineers. Federal, state, and local government agencies could be prime sources, particularly committees on employment of the so-called handicapped (employers consider it "good business" to hire qualified—not handicapped—persons).

Individuals as information sources include professionals and paraprofessionals engaged in related activities, such as school guidance and placement personnel, Employment Service personnel, and coworkers in counselors' own settings. Actual workers in prospective employment settings can provide "inside" information that is recent, if not necessarily reliable. Former clients now employed are often a ready source, willing and able to share pertinent information. One counselor organized a group of such persons to watch for possible job opportunities (Jeffrey, 1969, p. 25).

Employers themselves and their places of employment are obvious but distinctive sources. It is one thing to acquire information through conversations with employers, hiring personnel, or other employer personnel. Much of the information needed may be thus obtained. It is another thing to pay visits to places of employment and gain additional information through observation as well as conversation.

Depending on the size of the organization and other considerations, initial contact with an employer may be made at the hiring level or at a top executive level. The latter is favored by many experienced in placement, although it is often difficult and time consuming. It may also create resentment at the hiring level. Top management has wider latitude for special decisions, on the other hand, and its decisions will be followed at lower echelons.

Since employer relations are commonly discussed in placement literature (Jeffrey, 1969; *Manual on Selective Placement of the Disabled,* 1965), emphasis is given here on field visits to places of employment, with particular attention to informal job analysis and possible job modifications. Visits can verify information obtained from other sources and develop firsthand information otherwise not available. Many of the variables sampled under "Information about Employers"—some more subtle than others—are best assessed through personal visits.

Examples can be added to the sample to make the needed emphasis on the value of visits. The topography of the place of employment (hilly or level) and the location of the parking lot are observable. Ventilation and other physical factors may be found favorable in some parts of the plant, though not in others. The pace or tempo of work and other possible pressures can be observed, together with the characteristics of coworkers and supervisors.

To get at specific aspects of particular jobs, site visitors basically extend their observational skills into the area known as job analysis. Anxiety aroused in counselors by this term, if simply a "fear of the unknown," should be allayed by exposure to job analysis, mainly by doing it. Because it can be done without adopting a formidable formal format, the less threatening term "informal job analysis" has long been used by the author (1970). The threat is lessened further by knowing that one's own observation is supplemented by clarifying information elicited from workers and supervisors.

Counselor confidence in conducting informal job analysis is bolstered by helpful books on the subject. The U.S. Department of Labor's *Handbook for Analyzing Jobs* (1972) applies the *Dictionary of Occupational Titles'* (1965) worker functions (Data, People, and Things), worker traits (physical demands, environmental conditions, interests, temperaments, aptitudes, and training time), as well as materials, products, subject matter, services, machines, tools, equipment, and work aids. Informal job analysis, instead of being overwhelmed by so many variables, uses them selectively in relation to particular clients. For rehabilitation clients, a valuable aid to counselors is still the pioneering book by Hanman (1951).

To serve individual clients and to cut through often abstract job titles and general job descriptions to the individuality of actual jobs, any number of additional variables could be considered. Whatever the variables, they must be viewed within the content and the context of the job, without contamination by the capacities of the particular worker. Because a worker is using vision does not mean that a blind person could not perform the job. Because two arms are ordinarily used does not necessarily bar a one-armed person.

The limitations of clients must be distinguished, therefore, from the limitations of job analyses that set up unrealistic requirements. Even without job modifications, clients with severe disabilities can work at numerous jobs. In a 1973 vocational survey of fourteen business establishments, the author found that, out of 865 light or sedentary jobs, 498 could be performed by persons with a single upper limb. About 300 of these jobs involved use of the telephone, a sound instrument for effective placement.

Minor job modifications open up many more placement possibilities. Slight adjustments in working heights, machine controls, or work flow enable disabled persons to be effective employees. The completed work of a person with restricted mobility, for example, can be picked up by the worker at the next bench or desk. Other examples, as well as basic information about simple modifications of work tasks and work environments, are available in a number of sources (*Adaptation of Jobs for the Disabled,* 1973; Dahlke and Douglas, 1972; Garris, 1971; U.S. Civil Service Commission, 1972; U.S. Department of Labor, 1967, 1970).

Counselors and Placement

Familiarity with informal job analysis and possible job modifications, with information about employers and places of employment, with job placement strategies and placement counseling provides counselors with some fundamental knowledge on which to build placement expertise. Heightened expertise and lowered anxiety may not suffice, however, to engage counselors in an area toward which their attitudes are resistant. Placement involvement and placement effectiveness cannot be forced upon counselors.

While job placement is unquestionably an integral part of the vocational rehabilitation process, the question has constantly arisen as to whether it need be an integral part of rehabilitation counseling. A rationale can readily be offered for placement as something rehabilitation counselors themselves should do, as a function in addition to an underlying responsibility.

Doing placement keeps counselors in direct touch with the real world of employers and jobs that clients are being prepared to enter. Added realism can strengthen vocational planning, provided long-range perspective is not blurred by short-term or local job availability. Continuity of counseling through placement and postplacement services avoids fragmentation of functions—and of persons to whom clients must relate. The counseling relationship may be reinforced by the counselor's participation in placement (Jorgensen, et al., 1968).

Separation of the counseling and placement functions has also been justified, beyond the reluctance of many counselors to do placement. Not all counselors are capable of doing placement effectively, for two different sets of competencies may be involved. An efficient division of labor could serve clients better. Placement itself has increasingly become a specialization, with placement specialists employed in many vocational rehabilitation settings. Burress (1970, p. 6) proposed that the placement function be regarded

> as a service that is distinct from but at a level with rehabilitation counseling. Every effort should be made to endow this function as a profession with suitable remunerative and status rewards so as to attract recruits into the field who have the rare combination of interests, abilities, and orientations essential for this job.

The dilemma is not resolved by comparing the length of the two preceding paragraphs or by opting for the "truth" of one or the other rationale. The crucial thing is for clients to be provided effective placement services. Counselors are responsible to see that such services are provided, whether they perform the placement function themselves or placement specialists do so. Whoever does so is dependent upon a number of variables: the placement competence of particular counselors, agency services and staffing patterns, clienteles served and caseload sizes, and community placement resources. Job placement might be the job of whichever person can best serve an individual client.

BIBLIOGRAPHY

Adaptation of Jobs for the Disabled. Geneva, Switzerland: International Labour Office, 1973.

Burress, J. R. *Lou Ortale Memorial Lecture.* Washington, D.C.: The President's Committee on Employment of the Handicapped, 1970.

Dahlke, M. H. and Douglas, R. *Job Descriptions and Physical Demands Requirements with Job Restructuring for the Handicapped.* Milwaukee, Wisc. (6055 North 91st Street): Goodwill Industries of Wisconsin, 1972.

Flannagan, T. "What Ever Happened to Job Placement?," *Vocational Guidance Quarterly,* 22, 1974, 209-213.

Frank, D. S. "Group Counseling Benefits Jobseekers with Epilepsy," *Rehabilitation Record,* 9(1), 1968, 34-37.

Garris, A. G. "Technical Consultant for the Severely Disabled," *Rehabilitation Record,* 12(3), 1971, 15-18.

Hanman, B. *Physical Capacities and Job Placement.* Stockholm: Nordisk Rotogravyr, 1951.

Jeffrey, D. L. *Pertinent Points on Placement.* Stillwater, Okla.: Oklahoma State University, 1969.

Job Seeking Skills Reference Manual. Minneapolis, Minn. (1900 Chicago Avenue): Minneapolis Rehabilitation Center, 1971.

Jorgensen, G. Q., Janzen, F. V., Samuelson, C. O. and McPhee, W. M. *Interpersonal Relationships: Factors in Job Placement.* Salt Lake City: University of Utah, 1968.

Knape, C. S. "Placement: A Try-Out Experiment," *Journal of Rehabilitation,* 38(6), 1972, 29-32.

Manual on Selective Placement of the Disabled. Geneva, Switzerland: International Labour Office, 1965.

McClure, D. P. "Placement through Improvement of Clients' Job-Seeking Skills," *Journal of Applied Rehabilitation Counseling,* 3, 1972, 188-196.

Ninth Institute on Rehabilitation Services. *Placement and Follow-Up in the Vocational Rehabilitation Process.* Washington, D.C.: Rehabilitation Services Administration, 1972.

Olshansky, S., Grob, S. and Ekdahl, M. "Survey of Employment Experiences of Patients Discharged from Three State Mental Hospitals," in L. P. Blum and R. K. Kujoth, Eds., *Job Placement of the Emotionally Disturbed.* Metuchen, New Jersey: Scarecrow Press, 1972, pp. 404-421.

On-Job-Training Program Procedures Manual. Washington, D.C. (5530 Wisconsin Avenue): International Association of Rehabilitation Facilities, 1974.

Salomone, P. R. "A Client-Centered Approach to Job Placement," *Vocational Guidance Quarterly,* 19, 1971, 266-270.

Schneider, L. R., and Stevens, N. D. "Personality Characteristics Associated with Job-seeking Behavior Patterns," *Vocational Guidance Quarterly,* 19, 1971, 194-200.

Sheppard, H. L. and Belitsky, A. H. *Promoting Jobfinding Success for the Unemployed.* Kalamazoo, Mich. (300 South Westnedge Avenue): W. E. Upjohn Institute for Employment Research, 1968.

Sinick, D. "Educating the Community," *Journal of Rehabilitation,* 34(3), 1968, 25-27; 40.

Sinick, D. *Occupational Information and Guidance.* Boston: Houghton Mifflin, 1970.

Sinick, D. "Job Placement and Post-Placement Services for the Epileptic

Client," in G. N. Wright, Ed., *Epilepsy Rehabilitation,* Boston: Little, Brown, 1974, pp. 70-78.

Stevens, N. D., and Schneider, L. R. "The Dynamics of Job-seeking Behavior," *Journal of Employment Counseling,* 4, 1967, 56-62.

U.S. Civil Service Commission. *Handbook of Selective Placement.* Washington, D.C.: U.S. Government Printing Office, 1972.

U.S. Department of Labor. *Dictionary of Occupational Titles,* 3d ed., vol. II, *Occupational Classification.* Washington, D.C.: U.S. Government Printing Office, 1965.

U.S. Department of Labor. *Job Redesign for Older Workers: Ten Case Studies.* Washington, D.C.: U.S. Government Printing Office, 1967.

U.S. Department of Labor. *A Handbook for Job Restructuring.* Washington, D.C.: U.S. Government Printing Office, 1970.

U.S. Department of Labor. *Handbook for Analyzing Jobs.* Washington, D.C.: U.S. Government Printing Office, 1972.

Way, J. G., and Lipton, L. "An Employment Readiness Program for Young Veterans," *Vocational Guidance Quarterly,* 22, 1973, 64-66.

Zuger, R. R. "To Place the Unplaceable," *Journal of Rehabilitation,* 37(6), 1971, 22-23.

IMPLICATIONS FOR REHABILITATION PRACTICE

This chapter comes to grips with the disinclination of many rehabilitation workers to associate themselves professionally with job placement activities. In presenting a "strategies" approach to placement that requires high levels of professional understanding and expertise, the author rejects the notion that other aspects of rehabilitation are more demanding, fashionable, and rewarding. The placement function makes demands on rehabilitation workers for skillful counseling, an awareness of the complex psychodynamics of clients, employers, and counselors, an awareness of the occupational facts of life, and a sensitivity to the delicate three-way partnership that eventuates when client, counselors, and employer work together. It is contended that no matter who does the actual placement—the rehabilitation counselor, the rehabilitation specialist, or the clients, themselves—all involved require appropriate skills in performing their respective functions and all must play important roles.

The blame for the prevailing deemphasis on placement in the rehabilitation process has been placed variously on the counselor training institutions, on the agencies that differentiate placement from other types of rehabilitation counseling, and/or counselor self-perceptions as "hot-house" office workers who impact clients primarily through talking with them. Fixing the blame more specifically will not automatically restore placement to its rightful niche in vocational rehabilitation. A common axiom in the field is that rehabilitation counseling does not take place in a vacuum. On the contrary, it is conditioned by powerful social and economic forces that impinge upon counselor and client alike, even in the rarefied atmosphere of the counseling office. All too often counselees are brought by their counselors to the threshold of placement and are then deserted by their counselors, resulting in possible unemployment, frustration, and disappointment with the rehabilitation experience.

Client expectations, job accountability, and reality-based vocational counseling all demand that rehabilitation counselors perceive themselves as having a major, if not the central responsibility, for the successful job placement of their clients. Many agencies that have permitted their counselors to abdicate this responsibility, training institutions that have relegated placement courses and field experiences to a secondary position in the curriculum, and counselors who have perceived themselves largely as psychotherapists are beginning to tune in once again to the *vocational* side of vocational rehabilitation. Thus, the distinctive feature of vocational rehabilitation is becoming more emphasized and placement is less often the professional pariah of rehabilitation service. Some rehabilitation workers may continue to feel that they do not want to "soil their hands" with vocational placement concerns, but their vocational rehabilitation clients will continue to want a job above all else. In the long run counselors who really care about their vocational rehabilitation clients will move placement out of the shadows back into the forefront of rehabilitation service.

CHAPTER XII

SOME CHARACTERISTICS OF COMPREHENSIVE REHABILITATION TEAMWORK

SETTING THE SCENE

As rehabilitation becomes increasingly complex and as more clients with severe and complicated problems enter the rehabilitation process, the number of different disciplines participating in service programs is growing inexorably. When rehabilitation was younger and only three or four different professions participated in assisting a single client, the problems of welding even so small a group into an effective helping instrument were formidable. Today, when as many as ten or fifteen disciplines may conjointly serve one disabled individual, the number and dimensions of teamwork problems increase geometrically. The common consequences of inadequate teamwork are client confusion, overlap and duplication, interprofessional conflict, ill-defined roles, unduly high service costs, and overconcern with team dynamics rather than client welfare.

For many years, interdisciplinary rehabilitation teamwork was considered to be attainable through goodwill, concern for the patient, and faith in common sense. As these sources of teamwork failed to automatically insure effective interprofessional cooperation, a few rehabilitation specialists (most notably, Frederick Whitehouse, the author of this chapter) began to explore possibilities for arriving at a rational, theoretical, and practical base for bringing many disciplines together on behalf of an individual client. The roots of these insights extended into many fields including group dynamics, human personality, social group work, anthropology, social psychology, and sociology. At this point in the development of rehabilitation, directions toward improved teamwork are becoming clearer. In reading this chapter, one should be alert to possible solutions to such teamwork problems as: how roles of the contributing professions are defined, how an individual professional worker can have his effectiveness enhanced by participating in a team process, how the client can benefit from the combined and coordinated efforts of a multidisciplinary group, and what a team can do to maximize its strengths and effectiveness.

213

CHAPTER XII

SOME CHARACTERISTICS OF COMPREHENSIVE REHABILITATION TEAMWORK

Frederick A. Whitehouse

The subject of teamwork is both broad and complicated. This paper offers one subtopic in outline form. Since discussion of each item would result in great length, it is hoped that the readers will find them provocative to their own thinking and discussion with others.

As a preliminary it would be advisable to dwell briefly upon a definition.

Teamwork is a close, cooperative, democratic, multiprofessional union devoted to a common purpose—the best treatment for the fundamental needs of the individual. Its members work through a combined and integrated diagnosis; flexible, dynamic planning; proper timing and sequence of treatment; and balance in action. It is an organismic group distinct in its parts, yet acting as a unit, i.e., no important action is taken by members of one profession without the consent of the group. Just as the individual acts as an interrelated whole, and not as a sum of his characteristics, so must the professions act, think, interpret, and contribute toward a diagnosis which is the product of all, and a treatment plan which is dynamic to accommodate the changes which a dynamic human organism is constantly making. Rehabilitation group members require a firm foundation in one science, which must include a keen awareness of its limitations, an understanding of some of the fundamental philosophy, practices, and limitations of the companion and cooperating sciences, and an open, mature, flexible mind towards meeting new ideas and challenges. These members must feel secure in their own professions. Furthermore, members of such a group must not only be concerned for the welfare of the client, but also should be stimulated by the intellectual problem to be solved. A proper combination and balance of these two are essential. Teamwork provides postprofessional education on a broad base, and results in a higher professional performance for all, than any one could achieve alone. Each new member from an allied profession should mean not an arithmetical gain, but a geometrical one, since each member should influence and educate all. Administration in this setting must be democratic to allow free interplay of professional knowledge in the development of treatment. Without such freedom, the highest level of operation will never be reached (Whitehouse, 1951 A).

Characteristics of a Quality Team

Philosophy

(1) The client comes first under all conditions. Exigency, economic considerations, and administrative convenience are secondary. The client is the center not the profession, the team, or the facility establishment.

(2) The team has a democratic philosophy and democratic leadership and operates under a democratically administered facility (Whitehouse, 1951A; Stogdill, 1974).

(3) Respect is shown for the clinical freedom of each profession not only by the membership but by the administration in the setting. Clinical decisions are its professional business and responsibility. Services to the client are best defined by the team. It is not a function of administrative prerogative to interfere in any way.

(4) The team is creative and innovative because each client is recognized as unique. The dedication to such a quality obviously means that planned efforts for individualizing the client cannot be uniform and automatic but require imagination, daring, and even risk. Science and art join to form innovation. This attitude of creativity is also the basis for problem-solving (Gordon, 1961).

(5) There is an emphasis not only upon the quality of each service but on the total team's maximum effectiveness. "Teamwork is

a commitment to excellence" (Whitehouse, 1965). This is encouraged by the nature of the team's functioning (See Section B, Procedures and Methods).

(6) Goals are always comprehensive, that is, short cuts to an inferior rehabilitated status are not made (Whitehouse, 1953). It would deny its very purpose if just any mediocre solution is the goal. Compromise is made as a last resort only when higher-level goals prove not feasible.

(7) Since the team treats clients with complicated problems, once a client is accepted and reasonably complete rehabilitation not possible, an "augmentative philosophy" prevails in which whatever ability can be improved will be given service (Whitehouse, 1954). In some instances, beyond professional prognostication, the client improves over a long-time period. The team becomes acutely conscious that unless the client can be helped by comprehensive services that he may have no other recourse. This is not egotistical but real in the helping fields. A review, for example, of the previous efforts resulting in a voluminous case file of failure is frequent. Persistence and trial and retrial is usual. And enough success is found to justify this attitude.

(8) There is faith in the team and in its ability to perform in a superior fashion (Whitehouse, 1951B). A level of sophistication about human potential is achieved. The physician is no longer astonished that a client may perform physical feats he initially regarded as highly improbable. The psychologist accepts that a client may turn out to learn and apply himself well in spite of the discouraging implications of formal tests. The social worker long ago found that he may be fooled by clients who "talk a good game" but who do not or cannot buckle down to training. The rehabilitation counselor becomes accustomed to finding that a client's horizons may expand so much under concerted professional service that his original estimate has become embarrassingly gloomy. Consequently, a sense of humility also develops as each professional sees clearer the limitations of his work in the midst of so many other important contributors. It further leads one to the recognition that even with the extraordinary combined talent of a team that each profession is highly deficient.

(9) No one profession takes the "credit" but all share in the triumph of successful client rehabilitation and, on the other hand, whatever "failure" results is shared by all. It is recognized that some achievement is beyond a profession or a team.

(10) Frankness, openness, trust, acceptance, and an absence of seeking blame or denigration is characteristic. Friction is accepted as an inescapable issue in human relationships. Renewed efforts at understanding rather than bitterness and resentment is what is expected by fellow members. There is social pressure not to permit a personal feeling of injury to develop into antagonism. There are generally no "secrets" about errors, problems, or situations concerned with the client withheld from the team which in other settings might be private to the department. If for no other reason than that "secrets" usually become known anyway, and then tend to destroy credibility which is greatly needed because of the difficulty in fully understanding another discipline and in keeping conflict to a minimum. Primarily, however, it is because of team ethics. Sherif (1956) said, ". . . hostility gives way when groups pull together to achieve overriding goals which are real and compelling to all concerned."

(11) While structure, regulation, and organization are necessary, a common philosophy about teamwork is also essential; competence and experience are important, as well as a strong desire to serve with dedication. Nothing can help more to preserve the quality of the process and its accomplishments and to ease the inevitable frictions than confidence, trust, and positive feelings toward each other. Mackworth (1965) in speaking of multidisciplinary research says: "The success of such arrangements undoubtedly depends on the feeling of common purpose that can be developed so that the various individuals work together really effectively."

Whitehouse (1962) has proposed that teamwork as a process is a therapeutic growth experience for its members. It is evident that this thesis has the support of Gibb and Gibb (1968), who say in speaking of the value of a group:

A growing group moves toward the integration of group-determined goals. A member feels that his most significant goals are creatively achieved in the group, he does not sacrifice anything for the group, loses nothing by compromise or sacrifice or duty, and is able to feel fulfilled and satisfied by creative work towards goals that the total group has come to value. The healthy group is growing toward spontaneous and participative structure and function.

Procedures and Methods. Perhaps, the primary issue of team functioning effectively and efficiently lies in the nature of its leadership. However, who is to lead the leaders? Each professional should be capable of providing some degree of leadership. The members of such a body are best equipped to nominate their own leader or, upon a particular occasion, to call upon a member as especially qualified because of the nature of the business before it, as in the case of admissions or closure.

It is vital that the team decide who is to chair its meetings. Some individuals are good facilitators and are more open and sensitive to nuances that arise in a group. They are also prepared to assume some of the extra work connected with scheduling, checking, and arranging and to expedite or coordinate some of the decisions that require ongoing attention. Since it becomes an added task, the team might rotate the chair at specified periods. Some members may be reluctant to take upon added responsibilities or may not feel as competent for this job as others. Yet, it is usually an excellent learning experience that should not be bypassed. Brown (1963) quotes Henry Harris (1949) in an excellent statement:

> Leadership is a collective function: collective in the sense that it is the integrated synergized expression of a group's efforts: it can only arise in relation to a group problem or purpose; it is not the sum of individual dominances and contributions, it is their relationship. Insofar as man contributes to the collective leadership function . . . he will realize that the ultimate authority and true sanction for leadership, at every point where it is exercised, resides—not in the individual—but in the "total situation" and in the demands of that situation.

One problem is that the facility administrator may often either assume the role or designate an individual, frequently a physician.

This is particularly true in hospitals and other medically dominated settings. It might also occur in other institutions either automatically or possibly because the physician may happen to be a good democratic leader.

It may happen automatically because the physician demands the prerogative, and it is accepted because of the threat he poses which is discussed later. A physician may be convinced he should be the leader and this may be true in part of others, especially administrators, because he sees this function as a desirable status befitting his profession since medical training usually supports this view or because of his narrowness since he sees almost everything as a "medical problem." It is possible also that in good conscience he doesn't make distinctions but sees it as a natural right because of his "legal responsibility."

The mere raising of the phrase "legal responsibility" usually throws administrators and boards into unquestioned panic. Perhaps in the latter case this is a result of the frequent composition of an institutional board which may be made up of retired physicians, businessmen, and politicians.

Frequently the issue of "legal responsibility" for the patient is raised by medical workers in such a way that other team members almost automatically back off in awe. Yet, it is hardly worth serving human beings if our level of service is not based on professional ethics that transcend what is always the lowest common denominator—legality. If questioned about the morality of an act, we may expect the businessman to say: "Well,, it's legal."

Parents have legal responsibilities concerning their children but the law cannot force a parent to give or not give love to them. The realm at issue is not legal responsibility. All are legally bound in many ways, and we cannot do injury or subject a client to loss of privacy, and we cannot neglect duties which may result in another's loss. It is also clear that records of anyone may be subpoenad and anyone may be sued. Furthermore, besides the higher ethical responsibility of a profession beyond legal responsibility, we all have a personal ethical or moral level above even that to consider when the client's best interests are at stake.

The main basis for "control" then is self-discipline as well as the concerted body of members who comprise team discipline. No other means are necessary. In fact, breakdown of responsibility and ethics are *more* apt to occur under authoritarian control.

The team decides on a consensus basis, that is, votes are not taken on client treatment. They may be taken, of course, on policies that affect all clients or team procedures and methods.

A vote is evidence of a breakdown in communication—of failure to articulate issues—and results in a tyranny of the majority. It tends to be infectious so that in the future the easy way out is taken more readily and strategy to "win" becomes part of the game. Also, the mere issue of "taking a vote" is a clear indication of a lack of understanding not only of team philosophy but of professional responsibility to the client. Furthermore, a decision arrived at by vote is, of course, not necessarily the truth.

The team doesn't consider its "consensus" as sacred and beyond recall but gives every opportunity and reasonable time for those with reservations to develop their thesis by further trial or other measures. Since there must be a better solution than merely a majority version of an issue, continued refinements of positions are made.

Differences are especially apt to happen when considering case closure. In those favoring closure, it may be due to frustration with the client on the part of some service; a feeling that maximum benefit has been achieved; a belief that a particularly good work opportunity should not be passed even though more service could be given, or, a conviction that for some reason, the particular setting is not appropriate for the client, among other motives.

On the other hand, the retention opinions may be due to an over-emotional client advocacy, a feeling that closure would deprive the service of the "payoff" for their personal investment or, certainly, a strong intuition that client gain is in the offing. Professional opinion, regardless of the suspected illegitimacy of the basis, must be respected.

Parallels exist in the area of acceptance of a client. Often, clients can be offered services which some believe to be a waste of time. Usually, further information solicited or some trial will decide quickly. Nevertheless, these issues become increasingly part of the team's sophistication.

The team does not suppress competition. First of all, it cannot do so, as such an aspect will be present anyway, and it can be of value as it stimulates and motivates. Second, the real issue is the nature and degree of competition for it can be misused and disruptive. The prize to be fought for is the quality of service to the client, not power. It is competition against the unknown, against the barriers, rather than vying against one's fellows. One strives to be respected by other disciplines but even more to achieve a high degree of self-respect as having done one's best.

The team makes and regulates its own rules and procedures. It isn't only the issue of democratic control but of clinical freedom. Much of the professional's training has been categorical, with so many rules relating to one's chosen field. There aren't such restrictions set out in a team process; consequently, the high-level team is empiric and feels freer to make and to break its own regulations whenever it so determines.

Frequent submeetings take place as well as a multiplicity of informal exchanges. An outsider may have the naive view that teamwork is what takes place at the large regular meeting. While true in part, even more of the process takes place in multiple associations in the intervening periods.

Regularly scheduled meetings are held every so often for the purpose of self-education. On such occasions individual cases are not discussed but process, effectiveness, and discipline philosophy are reviewed. Each discipline has its own philosophy, its philosophy about rehabilitation and each individual, and a personal interpretation. Shared viewpoints are very valuable to understanding another's decisions and performances (Whitehouse, 1955).

Ekstein (1971) supports this thesis when he remarks: "In assessment procedures the team needs to be complemented by a constant reexamination of existing structure, procedures, theories, and outlines; . . ."

The team member performs on a higher professional level than under other circumstances (Whitehouse, 1951B). This is due not only to greatly increased information, but opportunity to focus upon the particular area of one's professional discipline.

Since the powers are combined, its goals are higher than what may be accomplished in less comprehensive settings since the team recognizes its power of achievement (A5-8). Difficult cases are its primary business professionally and such practice sharpens performance. In addition, such complicated cases justify the higher economic cost.

Finally, there are fewer errors made with the number of highly trained minds asking questions, weighing answers, and critically reviewing. When errors are made they are detected sooner and usually obviated quickly.

The team process is constantly maturing and growing in its effectiveness, as well as the satisfactions of its members due to the experiences and concerted efforts to improve functioning.

A team spirit of a high order develops. This is a rather undefinable state, but an acknowledged one and may be manifested in a number of ways. Each member respects another's professional conscience and opinions and trusts the other's disciplinary methods. Loyalty to the team decision is regarded as an ethical responsibility. If doubts arise or circumstances change, the individual relays such reservations for team consideration.

Compromises are frequent. The neophyte member tends to be "prerogative conscious," equating much with the ownership of his profession. Realization soon comes that most of such claimed privileges are specious and due primarily to the nature of one's training which implicitly or even explicitly assumes that its vantage is the central focus of all treatment.

It is quite obvious that there are some compromises that one may not make nor be expected to make. Yet, such stances somehow become less important as the issue is what serves the client not the prestige of the individual profession's "ownership."

Cooperation is indeed a poor and lesser description of its working method. Collaboration is better and synegetic still better, but organismic is the best description of the ideal interrelationship. Teams may exist at all these levels and their status is the result of many factors beginning with leadership, setting, and experience.

An experienced team has realized that the usual concepts of diagnosis and prognosis encourage the promotion of categorization and therefore may be static as well as offer traps in thinking. A recent statement of the Council for Exceptional Children recognizes this element:

> To further the understanding and servicing of such children, special educators as well as other educational personnel should eliminate the use of simplistic categorizing. . . . In identifying such children, special educators should be concerned with the identification of their educational needs, not with generalized labeling or categorizing of children (1971).

Furthermore, when a profession has tendered its opinion as a "diagnosis," there is a human propensity to protect and support the declaration. Consequently, the team desires a descriptive report which will contain information which is relatively secure as well as imaginative hypotheses and clinical hunches. In the latter case, such statements may be good clues to other professions.

The team professes to serve the whole individual. The gathering of evidence is never closed whether it be further investigation of the past history, repeating of previous tests, additional assessments and evaluations, progress reports from various treatment modalities, growth in psychotherapy, improvements in vocational competence, changes in family attitudes, expansion of recreational skills, social graces, new ideas, and possibilities arrived at by an individual member or as a result of subgroup meetings between various services.

Consequently, diagnoses and prognoses are fluid, dynamic, working hypotheses, not closed decisions. This method is certainly more difficult and less comfortable but surely more productive. The entire association of the client with the setting is a "living period" of evaluation in which more is constantly learned through professional contact, through observation, and because the passage of time multiplies opportunity.

The team recognizes the limitations of a strictly "scientific approach" and utilizes clinical intuition in a legitimate and necessary partnership. For example, it accepts the fact that each profession may use different methods of judging progress. In some disciplines more objective and quantitative measures are possible, while in others, such as the areas of counseling, clinical opinions must be allowed without "hard" evidence. Yet even in such an instance, it expects and receives descriptive interpretation to the extent possible. It furthermore does not disparage but supports the role of clinical intuition and clinical impression even in the professional disciplines which normally stress quantification guides.

Decisions are formulated with caution and since it is never quite sure of its decisions, the team continually reexamines and checks along with developing at least temporary or emergency alternatives (Herrold, Davitz, Fox, Lorge, 1953).

While frequently violated in the poorer teams, it grants little weight to professional opinions by those who haven't seen or spoken to the client professionally. The better team has found that a "paper" opinion not only often misses something of significance but even at times misses something of critical import.

The client is as well informed as is possible. Major decisions about himself are his prerogative in spite of well-intentioned professionals. Questions are raised frequently as to the client's understanding and feelings about projected and ongoing services. Furthermore, the group gives serious deliberation to a client's request for a service which the discipline believes is not needed or not needed any longer. For example, there is the client who has reached maximum return in physical therapy but wishes to continue. Or, some clients may be continued temporarily until the psychic and emotional issues are resolved while others may need to face the reality now. Mere acceptance as "not doing any harm" is serving professional utility more than the client's best interests.

Besides a careful, thorough, and detailed assessment, a therapeutic strategy is devised which employs a selected sequence and coincidence of services; provision for modulation of emphasis; the institution of critical check points; possible shifting degree of responsibility; and the creation of multiple alternatives and efforts to increase client options.

It also looks ahead into the client's future in light of his past and current problems, that is, it views the client from a life continuum position so that it may not only orient its present actions but by extrapolation provide the client with long-term strengths insofar as this is possible and foreseeable.

Team evaluation of the client under most circumstances does not rely upon previous external findings and test results which are often performed and interpreted by those not acquainted with rehabilitation nor with comprehensive approaches. Time passage, the unknown quality of the reporter, errors in transmission, and other factors usually mean that a team does its own examination, testing, and observation to ensure accuracy.

To strengthen and to correct team opinions, members find numerous occasions for personal observation of the client in his other engagements in the setting (Whitehouse, 1951C; Whitehouse, 1969). Multiplicity of observations has always been a mark of science, and it must be also of good clinical procedures. This topic is worthy of much discussion.

The team does not rush to close a case out of frustration with a difficult client because the "house of cards" triumph of a risky case may be lost; by the reason that most services see no future; due to the referring agency's withdrawal of support; or on account of many other reasons which reflect more upon the deficiencies of the team than the client. These are often natural human failings which are sometimes hidden under other guises or tacitly agreed to. Time and work pressures affect every group and the result is a cause of error.

There is a strong sense of relevance to the community. The community to which the client must return, face, cope with, and live. This is to balance the tendency of intellectuals to contrive plans which may not fit the reality of client circumstance. This is a real problem especially since many professionals have gone from long academic involvement and professional training directly into professional practice. Their world is not the world of the client.

No system is logical unless it includes feedback. The team, in an effort to inspect its possible errors or deficiencies, institutes a well-planned follow-*through* of its closed cases *whether they were "rehabilitated" or not.* Such efforts often will locate a client reaching a critical point of some loss which may be rectified and also hopefully indicate what errors might have been made. Absence of this is usually blamed upon funds, but the major reason is the human propensity not to be robbed of satisfactions, and in fact, to find in some instances that team efforts were "wasted."

The team makes a major effort not to be influenced by time pressure and numbers of clients. There is a point at which all efforts for excellence collapses. And, on the other hand, there is the reality of economic cost. Balance of such factors will continue to be a problem in the foreseeable future of human service.

Insistence upon an appropriate physical location for its meetings is not an immature desire for prestige. A location of privacy, one not adversely affected by sights, sounds, and emblematic seating arrangements which infer hierarchy is required. Makeshift provisions do not enhance a climate of productivity. When it does happen, it is clear that both the administration and the team do not consider the task to be too serious. The team respects its work and should require administrative respect. It is more than comfort, it is symbolic of its commission (Hall, 1966; Thass-Thienemann, 1968).

Typically, the fine team is seldom careless about starting on time, canceling meetings, cutting them short, or permitting interruptions.

Pertinent to the latter, its meetings are not a showcase for the establishment. It seldom welcomes visitors because such intrusions may alter what may or could be said and also out of respect for the client. Such outsiders, depending upon their nature, will influence the group sometimes subtly as well as in obvious ways.

Communication

The quality team communicates in a superior fashion as each member acquires a broader professional knowledge and vocabulary through association, and an increased appreciation of the personal nuances of others from a verbal as well as nonverbal reception. Furthermore, since there are so many professional standpoints, one learns how essential it is to present information with clarity, accuracy, and coherence to obtain understanding from others (Whitehouse, 1965). Ruesch (1961) in speaking of the scientist working on a team says:

> He meets communication difficulties of three distinct kinds: first, the vicissitudes of personal contact, when different backgrounds meet. Second, the confusions which arise because the data are expressed in words. (Any vocabulary is based upon specific underlying assumptions and rules of interpretation which are not transferable to another vocabulary . . .). And, third, the conceptual difficulties which make their appearance when a theory of theories has to be created to combine the concepts and findings of the various sub-disciplines.

The recognition that the problem of communication is a basic and exceptional problem is held without question. It is a dominant theme in the literature in interprofessional relations. In fact, as Fremont-Smith (1953) has put it: "The problem of communication between disciplines we feel to be a very real and urgent one, the most effective advancement of the whole of science being to a large extent dependent upon it."

The arbitrary territories which have divided the human being and condition, and which we call professions need vitally a means such as teamwork to assemble and to integrate the aspects.

Spinoza said: "Things that have nothing in common with each other cannot be understood by each other mutually; the conception of the one does not include the conception of the other." It is clear that overlapping of knowledges not only serves as a bridge to understanding but, even more, permit opportunity for minor contribution in another field when appropriate circumstances argue for such performance.

Depending upon the quality of the team, it doesn't just "report," it doesn't only "communicate," but it "communes," that is, it offers something beyond professional language however well articulated but transfers also feelings, nuances, intuitions, attitudes, and hopes about the issues (Whitehouse, 1970). Such offerings seldom take place in an atmosphere of mistrust or authoritarian control because it makes individuals feel too vulnerable.

Information as far as is possible is exchanged face-to-face. The poorer team takes refuge in barrages of memos some of which are not understood and which never fully convey as much as an interpersonal discussion. Of course, such written statements are necessary, but they require supplementation by personal interchange because more can be transmitted and exchanged by such teams (Whitehouse, 1967). Also, when reporting, individuals speak to the group not to the leader only and when commenting, individuals speak to the member whose statements stimulated the comments. Obviously, there are exceptions.

Reporting is honest and unafraid in its content. The poorer team reports tend to be protective, cautious, and negative. No risks are taken which might fail. Sometimes a deliberately dismal prospect is offered so that everything that happens subsequently will be praiseworthy. There are even those who feel that pessimism is a professional plus since it is supposed to be scientific and objective. While optimism has its disappointments, it leads toward greater accomplishment in the long run.

In addition, a statement about the client is never just put forth as a decision or conclusion without the reasoning behind the offering. Sometimes the reasoning is not well constituted and other members may see flaws that the presenter does not. On other occasions, the speaker will admit that it is a clinical impression. It may not be easy to lay bare our judgments but such practice in the long run is constructive and beneficial to professional exchange.

The better team is deeply concerned about the valuable time of its members and the proper use of time at its conferences. Its reports are available before its meetings for two reasons: first, so that they need not be given verbally in long statements and the time spent will mainly be on interpretation, answering questions and discussion; and second, so that the other members may have an opportunity to review, reflect, and prepare questions for the meeting. A series of verbal report readings are not only boring but points may be missed and questions avoided about what was already clearly stated.

A poorer team usually has lengthier reports which cover a disproportionate time of the meeting. Lengthier perhaps because of a vying for prestige ("see how thorough we are," "see what effort we take," etc.); a play for greater control of the client by the size impression of the report; a defensive measure to wear down and inhibit questions about the report, or, merely because of carelessness. The quality team spends proportionately greater time in discussion, "thinking out loud" and in review.

There are less private conversations at meetings; less appearance of boredom; more spontaneity and attention; responsiveness to another's statement; more looking at each other; a relative absence of private nods and smiles; less sarcasm and irony; less voice raising and less rush to end the meeting because one always has "something more important to do."

As experience grows, members learn what kinds of information other services than their own may regard as significant and therefore may offer observational accounts which they themselves do not believe can be appreciated by their own profession. There is no tolerance for the "bombshell" report. If something of great significance is to be brought up, the services concerned are notified ahead of time. Such actions are childish and either are done for prestige or vindictiveness. In any case, it is destructive, not likely to occur with a fine team and if it did, censure would be united against the perpetrator.

Ambiguity and contrary information is accepted as an inevitable factor in clinical affairs as it is in individual practice. This may be seen especially in the initial presentation of findings toward which considerable tolerance must be shown. With a quality team it is seldom due to slipshod work but the nature of an open-minded system not to discard discrepancies until further checking. In time, at least the major inconsistencies are resolved. Yet, the poor team in its insecurity doesn't tolerate this well and tends to force opinions and demand answers in "procrustean bed" fashion since it fears to operate with uncertainty.

The more experienced a team, the more the reporting of client gains is not necessarily assumed to be due to their individual ministrations. The confidence gained, for example, by a client who now can cross the avenue on his own may be demonstrated with more flourish in another service. Improved family relations which required considerable effort by the social case worker may be reflected in improved attitudes toward employment. All take pleasure and satisfaction in client improvement. Often, on a poor team one may find that the one who happens to speak first will have already laid claim. Exchanges then become ploys toward "winning."

Membership

The quality team utilizes each member at his/her highest functional competence, that is, what each can do best and are trained to do. Unless a circumstance particularly requires it, one leaves what can better be done by someone else to someone else, and this is seen as logical and ethical. Whose purpose does it serve, the professional or the client, when physicians talk about jobs, physical therapists about family problems, psychologists about recreational pursuits, social case workers about vocational interests, and rehabilitation counselors about what may be good exercises? When the professional formerly worked more independently, he usually had, with all good intentions, acquired some habits which he felt were helpful to the client but these actions are now better performed by another (Ausubel, 1956).

Team members as far as possible are employed full time not only to provide better personal service to the client, increased opportunity for client observation, a chance for additional exchange with other members but also to increase their professional focus upon the purposes of the team and its mission.

Since the team which is exceptional has tended to retain its members, it has had long experience as a unit. There is a reasonable balance between the sexes and minority groups since life experience of many kinds add to the professional input of intelligence. Furthermore, clients obviously come from all groups and a team with a variety of backgrounds may offer better interpretation and relationship.

The more expert team usually has members with substantial previous experience in their fields as well as an earlier acquaintance with a team operation. The importance of factors other than professional competence is recognized in replacing a member. Personality, philosophy, and appropriate fit into the team are more important than the mere purchase of an individual wearing the badge of a profession (Zander, Cohen, and Stotland, 1957; Whitehouse, 1955). The quality team typically finds its work interesting, satisfying, and fulfilling. Its members appear happy with their work, and some firmly believe that there is nothing to do anywhere that compares with their current occupation. The practice offers extraordinary individual growth and the assocation becomes a therapeutic experience (Whitehouse, 1962).

Conclusion

The multidiscipline team has been referred to as "... the most powerful of all problem-solving tools" (Planning Research Corporation, 1969). Certainly, it is complicated and the literature encompasses all the professional fields involved. Perhaps, our highly competitive culture is one reason why each profession tends to reflect in the literature an assumption of its role as central. Robert Browning's long poem, "The Ring and the Book," offers ten different versions of the same occurrence from individual personal viewpoints. An account by each member of a team of a successful case would vary in their interpretations, with the real truth unknown. At the Battle of Salamis in 480 B.C., after the Greeks defeated the enemy fleet, they took a vote on which man showed the most valor. They couldn't agree, but they were unanimous in voting second prize to Themistocles. Perhaps the only concordance of a team would be that the general key was the teamwork process.

Besides the obvious and more dramatic issues of role relationships and group processes in a multidiscipline group, there are the more hidden problems of definitions (Borsodi, 1967), of causality (Bunge, 1963), and of language differences (Thass-Thienemann, 1973). Consider, for example, the fact that all professions do some kind of "counseling," and yet it is difficult for another profession to appreciate other forms than their own—in essence because of the philosophic base of each which supports and determines the nature of its functioning.

While not speaking of the comprehensive rehabilitation team, the following quotation by the eminent creator of cybernetics, Norbert Wiener, is germane:

We had dreamed for years of an institution of independent scientists, working together in one of these backwoods of science, not as subordinates of some great executive officer, but joined by the desire, indeed by the spiritual necessity, to understand the region as a whole, and to lend to one another the strength of that understanding (1948).

BIBLIOGRAPHY

Ausubel, D. P. "Relationships Between Psychology and Psychiatry: The Hidden Issues," *American Psychologist,* 1956, 2: 99-105.

Borsodi, Ralph *The Definition of Definition.* Boston: Porter Sargent, 1967.

Brown, J. A. C. *The Social Psychology of Industry.* Baltimore, Md.: Pelican Books, 1963.

Bunge, Mario. *Causality.* New York: World Publishing, 1963.

Council For Exceptional Children. "Basic Commitments and Responsibilities to Exceptional Children," *The Council.* Arlington, Va.: 1971.

Ekstein, Rudolf. "The Achilles Heel of the Team Process, Review of Disturbed Children: Examination and Assessment Through The Team Process". *Psychiatry and Social Service Review,* 1971, 5: 27-28.

Freemont-Smith, Frank in George Stevenson, Ed. *Administrative Medicine, Transactions of the First Conference,* March 9-11, 1953, 2V. New York: Josiah Macy Foundation, 1953.

Gibb, J. R. and Gibb, Lorraine M. "Leaderless Groups: Growth-Centered Values and Potentialities," in Herbert Otto and John Mann, *Ways of Growth,* New York: Grossman, 1968, pp. 101-114.

Gordon, W. J. J. *Synetics: The Development of Creative Capacity.* New York: Harper, 1961.

Hall, Edward T. *The Hidden Dimension.* Garden City, N.Y.: Doubleday, 1966.

Harris, Henry. *The Group Approach to Leadership-testing.* London: Routledge, 1949.

Herrold, K. F., Davitz, J., Fox, D. and Lorge, I. "Difficulties Encountered in Group Decision Making," *Personality and Guidance Journal,* 1953, 31: 516-523.

Mackworth, N. W. "Originality," *American Psychologist,* 1965, 20: 51-66.

Planning Research Corporation. "Interactions of Diverse Disciplines," *Scientific American,* 1969, 221: 18 (July).

Ruesch, Jurgen. "Psychosomatic Medicine and the Behavioral Sciences," *Psychosomatic Medicine,* 1961, 23: 277-286.

Sherif, Muzafer. "Experiments in Group Conflicts," *Scientific American,* 1956, 195: 54-58 (November).

Stogdill, R. M. *Handbook of Leadership: A Survey of Theory and Research.* New York: Free Press, 1974.

Thass-Thienemann, T. *The Interpretation of Language,* Vol. 1. *Understanding The Unconscious Meaning of Language.* New York: Jason Aronson, 1973.

Ibid. *Symbolic Behavior.* New York: Washington Square Press, 1968.

Whitehouse, Frederick A., "Response to Symbolic Stimuli: The Subtlety of Interpersonal Exchange," presented at 77th Annual Meeting, American Psychological Association, 1969. Abstract in *Proceedings of Meeting,* pp. 775-776, *American Psychological Association,* 1970.

Ibid. "Some Professional Concepts," in D. Malikin and H. Rusalem, Eds., *Vocational Rehabilitation of the Disabled.* New York: New York University, 1969, pp. 245-273.

Ibid. "The Language of the Body," *Hofstra Review,* 1968, 3, 28-33. Reprinted in *J. Coll. and University Person.,* 1969, 20, 25-32. Excerpted in *Personnel Management Communications Bulletin,* 23, Englewood Cliffs, N.J.: Prentice-Hall, 1969.

Ibid. "Tuning In and Tuning Out: Human Communication Networks," *Distinguished Lecture Series,* Hofstra University, Dec. 4, 1967.

Ibid. "Teamwork as A Dynamic System," *Cleft Palate Journal,* 1965, 2: 16-27.

Ibid. "Teamwork as A Therapeutic Experience," presented at Institute For Medical Social Workers, Association of Rehabilitation Facilities of Upstate New York, Albany, April 26, 1962.

Ibid. "Professional Teamwork" (Shorter version of "Teamwork, Some Questions and Problems," National Conference on Social Welfare, Philadelphia, Pa.: May 22, 1957), in *Proceedings of the National Social Welfare Forum,* 1957, pp. 148-157.

Ibid. "Teamwork, Philosophy and Principles," *Social Work Practice in Medical Care and Rehabilitation Settings,* Monograph II, American Association of Medical Social Workers, Washington, D.C. 1955, pp. 1-19.

Ibid. "The 'Augmentative' Approach to Habilation," *Cerebral Palsy Review* 1954, 15: 11-13.

Ibid. "Teamwork, Clinical Practice in Rehabilitation," *Exceptional Children,* 1953, 19: 143-153.

Ibid. A., "Teamwork, A Democracy of Professions," *Exceptional Children,* 1951, 18: 45-52. Reprinted *Readings in Rehabilitation Counseling,* C. H. Patterson, Ed. Champaign, Ill.: Stipes, 1960.

Ibid. B., "Teamwork, An Approach to a Higher Professional Level," *Exceptional Children*, 1951, 18: 75-82.

Ibid. C., "Vocational Training in a Rehabilitation Center," Part I, *Journal of Rehabilitation*, 1951, 17: 3-8. Part II, *Journal of Rehabilitation*, 1951, 17: 19-23.

Wiener, Norbert. *Cybernetics or Control and Communications in the Animal and the Machine.* New York: Wiley, 1948.

Zander, Alvin, Cohen, A. R., and Stotland, Ezra. *Role Relations in the Mental Health Professions.* Ann Arbor, Mich.: University of Michigan, Institute for Social Research, 1957.

IMPLICATIONS FOR REHABILITATION PRACTICE

The story is told of the rehabilitation team which spent months discussing alternatives for rehabilitating a severely disabled person. These lengthy interchanges dealt with such issues as who should do what to whom and when, what part each field should play in the doing, and how the group should ascertain if in the course of doing "it" the disabled individual was, indeed, moving toward desired goals. Despairing of the delay, the client finally gave up on the team and rehabilitated himself. Perhaps, in this case, the outcome was unexpectedly positive. More commonly, however, less resourceful clients give up in the face of delay and indecision and fall back into the less productive status of dependence, idleness, and hopelessness.

This article articulates some fundamentals of sound interdisciplinary teamwork and suggests criteria and characteristics which are useful in shaping such teamwork. Briefly, these include: (1) seeing the client as at the center of the rehabilitation process; (2) teamwork has to be led democratically with respect for every professional member's contribution; (3) team effectiveness has to be valued, along with the quality of each service offered; (4) comprehensive goals reflecting the total team's effort should be set if the rehabilitation process is to be successful; and (5) frankness, openness, trust, acceptance, and an avoidance of blame and denigration is characteristic of good team function. Equally important, however, is the presentation of a humanistic perspective of teamwork, designed for, and measured by, its impact upon the rehabilitation client. In this view, teamwork is measured not only in terms of the degree to which it fulfills a professional's vision of a "community" of scientists but, even more cogently, the benefits which it delivers to those whom it serves. In brief, one can have a finely honed team that helps clients passingly well and a more ad hoc interdisciplinary group that consistently yields optimum benefits for its clients.

The practical matter is that of assessing a team by observing its contributions to disabled and disadvantaged human beings rather than some abstract yardstick. If a team falls short on the client's outcome criterion, it should be altered in personnel, procedures, philosophy, or structure, then reassessed and altered again and again until client objectives are met most of the time. In brief, a beautiful team is known by its beautiful clients. Most often, a team becomes beautiful by following the principles stipulated by Dr. Whitehouse.

PART III

SUMMING UP

CHAPTER XIII

OLD PROBLEMS SEEKING
NEW SOLUTIONS

Herbert Rusalem and David Malikin

As the American rehabilitation movement settles into middle age, it is seeking to preserve its hard-won programs, funding, and traditions by adopting an enlightened conservatism that has important implications for innovation and experimentation. Evidence of this conservatism appears in:

- the monotonous, imperfect sameness of almost all current rehabilitation programs, most of them cast in the mold of respected and long-standing rehabilitation "truths."
- the enshrinement of certain rehabilitation components long before they merit deification, such as work sample evaluation, personal adjustment training, and face-to-face counseling.
- the persistence in worship of the state agency coordinating model to such a degree that competing systems are effectively throttled and kept from developing.
- the rigid adherence to the primacy of vocational objectives in the federal-state, and consequently, the voluntary agency rehabilitation system.
- the almost exclusive fixation on providing therapeutic services to disabled individuals when society is at least as much the patient and needs the therapy even more.
- the medical rehabilitation model, developed primarily for the physically handicapped, uncritically imposed on the intellectually, emotionally and socially disabled.
- the measurement of rehabilitation success in terms of numbers of

cases closed regardless of the severity of the conditions dealt with,
rather than the quality of service that went into those closures.
- the replacement of an earlier rehabilitation leadership style that
featured adventuresome problem-solving, by one that stresses
caretaking and bookkeeping.

During the past generation or so, there have been virtually no really
new rehabilitation service breakthroughs although research findings
and creative thinking have provided numerous leads. The administrative and counselor superstructure of the field has hardened to a
degree that divergent ideas penetrate only with great difficulty. Prac-
titioner job satisfaction and rewards generally are not based upon
revamping the system to make it significantly more responsive to
current conditions and needs, but upon conformity to the well-worn
and not altogether functional approaches of the past. In addition,
cracks are appearing in the system that make the essentially conservative leadership of this field increasingly anxious and, concurrently,
increasingly defensive and resistant to needed change.

There are numerous signs that the old forms are beginning to
crumble in the face of changing social and political conditions and that
additional "Band-Aid" interventions will hold off the eventual breakdown of the system for only a limited period of time. A longitudinal
view of the situation suggests that fundamental modifications in rehabilitation organization and practice have not and are not occurring
with sufficient rapidity to restore rehabilitation to the status it once
enjoyed during its Golden Age of the 1950s and 1960s. Indeed, the
price to be paid for "holding the line" may be felt in the field falling
farther and farther behind as it attempts to keep pace with these
troubled times.

Evidences of strains in the system appear in the continuing exacerbation of the following problems:

(1) Rehabilitation funding is becoming more precarious and less
     lavish every year.
(2) Well-intentioned efforts to reach almost all disabled persons
     with an appropriate rehabilitation service are not achieving
     planned objectives.
(3) The medical or therapeutic model that worked so well with

the physically handicapped in the past is growing less relevant for the intellectually, emotionally, and socially disabled.

(4) Society's acceptance of the disabled on a peer level is not growing to any substantial degree.

(5) With continuing high rates of unemployment among the nondisabled, the incidence of joblessness among the handicapped is rising rather than declining.

(6) Current residential environments, especially in urban areas, continue to thwart and defeat many disabled persons.

(7) Rehabilitation continues to talk interminably about public attitudes toward the handicapped but concerted action to reshape such attitudes remains on a primitive level.

(8) Despite efforts to place greater emphasis on the social and psychological domains of rehabilitation, *vocational* rehabilitation continues to dominate the field owing to federal support of employment-oriented programs.

(9) Although it is still too early to estimate the impact upon service to homebound, institutionalized, and other severely disabled persons of the Rehabilitation Acts of 1973 and 1974, as this is being written, the neglected and deprived status of these client subgroups appears as compelling as ever.

(10) A problem that is rapidly assuming major proportions in our society is that of large numbers of children and young adults who for a variety of reasons appear deficient in the learning of educational and vocational skills. Although many are also physically or emotionally handicapped, their learning disabilities often receive only minor attention from rehabilitation workers. While the fields of Education and Psychology have been investing considerable research talent and effort to gain more knowledge of how people learn, and are devising new teaching strategies to cope with learning deficits, the rehabilitation establishment seems hardly affected by this problem. An example of this unconcern is the action of the *Journal of Rehabilitation* in rejecting an article describing an experimental learning capacities program conducted at the Federation of the Handicapped Agency. This avoidance of significant learning issues and developments offers additional evidence that the *Journal of Rehabilitation,* a once vital, professional

organ, is turning into a publication of banal, sentimental material that will further devitalize the rehabilitation movement.

(11)   Although peer interventions have been selectively effective in treating alcoholics and drug addicts, a systematic understanding and use of such interventions for the rehabilitation of other disability groups has barely penetrated current programmatic practices.

(12)   Massive groups of disabled persons are receiving minimal rehabilitation services despite demonstration projects that clearly indicate the feasibility and desirability of offering rehabilitation assistance to them. Among these subgroups are: aging persons, preschool and school-age children, the homebound, the learning disabled, the neurologically impaired, the multihandicapped, and the culturally different.

(13)   Although there has been marked recent progress in deinstitutionalizing disabled persons, all too often this has been accomplished by administrative fiat that virtually expels them from their sheltered residences without adequate preparation for community living, rather than equipping such persons properly to cope with a new and more demanding community environment.

(14)   A large majority of rehabilitation case closures are attained through stereotyped evaluation, training, and placement programs that are characterized by routine thinking and perseveration rather than by responsiveness to the idiosyncratic needs, capacities, and interests of disabled individuals. Routine automatization rather than creativity permeates too much of today's rehabilitation practice.

(15)   Administrator and counselor accomplishments are too frequently measured in terms of the number of clients served, not in terms of the quality of such services. Thus, the client who gives promise of quick, "uncomplicated," and low-risk rehabilitation success is valued by many rehabilitation workers more highly than the very severely disabled person who requires additional time, effort, and imagination. With the rehabilitation reward system tied to numbers, quality is not afforded the ultimate priority it merits.

The prevalence of these problems suggests that the current rehabilitation system is in need of a major overhaul. The commonly stated argument to the effect that all that is needed to revitalize it is more money, more staff, and more facilities to perpetuate and extend the present system in virtually unchanged form is open to serious question. Alternately, it should be recognized that not money alone, nor personnel alone, nor facilities alone are likely to be a panacea. For example, the attenuated currently surviving antipoverty programs that had been launched with such bright hopes and plentiful funds in the 1960s are faltering almost everywhere, suggesting that attempts to solve social problems with lots of public dollars but little creativity, leadership, and risk-taking can be futile. The antipoverty program did not fail only because of the lack of dollars but also because inventive and viable solutions were either not available or not accepted. So it is with rehabilitation. The current need is for an infusion of new ideas that generate a revitalized excitement and willingness to experiment since only new concepts and approaches will enable us to break out of the shibboleths and dogmas that hold rehabilitation in restraints today.

New ideas are needed to cope with the 15 troublesome areas presented below. Suggestions are offered not because these suggestions constitute the only promising avenues for change. On the contrary, other equally relevant concepts merit equal consideration. Thus, the ideas that appear on the pages that follow were evolved to stimulate discussion rather than offer definitive answers. For a variety of reasons—such as political expediency, individual fearfulness, lack of positive leadership, perseveration, organizational arteriosclerosis, and unimaginative thinking—some of these ideas have either been overlooked or discarded prematurely. Readers of this book are urged to put aside personal bias, insofar as possible, and take a closer look at these notions, not merely through intellectual and emotional ruminations but through trying at least a few of them in daily practice even if in limited situations. Professional workers can find many reasons for *not* moving in new directions. Perhaps, through considering these ideas, individually and in groups, rehabilitation workers may open themselves increasingly to emergent concepts that hold promise for improved service to disabled persons in the future.

1. The Funding Problem. Present-day means of funding rehabilitation programs seem to have reached a plateau. Should we press for a social security system that provides Americans with assured funding for rehabilitation from the cradle to the grave through the medium of insurance payments as we now do in relation to retirement income? Should the funds provided under such an insurance system be paid directly to the consumers of such service for self-selected purchase of services as contrasted to the use of state agency middlemen?

2. The Hard-to-Find, Hard-to-Serve Disabled Person. Hundreds of thousands, perhaps millions, of disabled persons who could benefit from rehabilitation services are not gaining access to such services. Should we mandate periodic physical, emotional, intellectual, and social diagnostic examinations for American citizens? Should the findings of such examinations be screened (as in Social Security Disability Programs) to ascertain rehabilitation needs, readiness, and potential?

3. The Therapeutic Model Problem. Early rehabilitation programs addressed themselves primarily to physically handicapped persons, with important inputs being provided by physicians who, in time, stamped the field with the medical therapy model that now prevails. This model is most appropriate in situations in which attempts are made to therapeutically change the individual for the better. Should the now-dominant therapeutic approach be challenged to include other models that emphasize strategies for survival or the reshaping of the environment to make it more compatible with individual needs? Should we remake the disabled person or the disabled society that engulfs us all; which should be assigned the higher priority?

4. The Advocacy Problem. The status of any group in our society is related to its organizational cohesiveness and aggressiveness. Handicapped persons have not yet approached that level of organization that would enable them to compete with other groups for governmental funds, interest, and encouragement. Should we continue the current pallid and uncoordinated professional efforts to serve as advocates for the disabled? Should we form aggressive groups of rehabilitation workers, or should we train disabled persons themselves to man the barricades on their own behalf? Up to the present, professional workers have exhibited ambivalence in this area in that as conservative members of the establishment they have not been able to mount a concerted establishment-disturbing advocacy campaign for disabled persons and yet in their detachment, they concurrently recognize the need for organized and militant effort.

5. The Unemployment Problem. Even our most gifted economists seem to be perplexed by the current conditions in which high prices are maintained while purchasing power and employment decline. If this nation ever solves its critical economic dilemmas, the disabled will benefit as well as all other citizens. In the meantime, disabled individuals are competing with millions of nondisabled unemployed persons for existing jobs, a competition that places them at an evident disadvantage. If, indeed, all Americans, disabled or not, merit suitable job opportunities, how shall we assure the employment rights of the handicapped in periods of high unemployment? Shall jobs in government-guaranteed public service and public works be made available to all disabled persons who elect to work? Should industry be required by government to hire a certain proportion of disabled persons? Or should government-purchase activities be extended, simplified, and expanded so that more long-term workshop job slots can be created for those who cannot find work in competitive industry?

6. The Special Environment Problem. The demands of normal living environments, especially in urban areas, often lie beyond the adaptive capacities of non-disabled persons. The demands of these environments can be even more excessive on handicapped persons who may be more vulnerable to exploitation, violence, poverty, destructive competition, and interpersonal conflict than others in our society. Up to this point, integration of the disabled into unsheltered society has been a cherished hope of American rehabilitation workers. Have the inherent difficulties built into restrictive urban environments become so pronounced that integration goals, once hallowed, now are hollow? The well-documented debilitating effects of institutionalization suggest that a highly segregated setting can also be damaging. Can and should we design alternative partially segregated but challenging environments for certain severely disabled persons who are candidates for neither the rigors of unsheltered living nor institutionalization? Should we explore the kibbutz, commune, or colony idea, specialized segregated apartment houses, the hostel, or the semisheltered residence, or should we set up "new towns," country estates and individual or group homes for the handicapped persons who cannot cope with community conditions?

7. The Problem of Attitude-Shaping. Most observers agree that negative public attitudes and behaviors constitute one of the most serious drawbacks to community, family, and job parity for disabled persons. Current efforts to change such attitudes and behaviors are spotty, haphazard, uncoordinated, and futile. Has the time come to mount an organized massive public education campaign to help Americans to view handicapped persons more favorably? If such a campaign is mounted, should it be placed in the hands of canny and sometimes devious Madison Avenue types who get results, or should it be kept in the hands of professional rehabilitation workers who, regardless of their other virtues, are relatively inept in this public relations field?

8. The Vocational Emphasis Problem. The present federal-state rehabilitation system and its network of associated voluntary rehabilitation programs is still largely tied to the requirement of setting and pursuing a vocational objective. Since the vocational rehabilitation emphasis has proven itself by every test for more than 50 years, should it be retained unmodified in its present differentiated form? Should it be kept as it is now but expanded and enriched by new ideas, or should it be substantially modified to adapt it to better meet the needs of the large mass of disabled persons for whom psychosocial rather than vocational rehabilitation is more appropriate? Would incorporating social rehabilitation into the current service structure render the present vocationally oriented system impotent so that the allegedly "easier" social rehabilitations will "drive out" the more difficult vocational rehabilitations? Is the solution to be found in the form of a parallel, coordinated, but autonomous social rehabilitation system that maintains different admissions and success criteria and provides differentiated services and approaches to the rehabilitation problems of severely disabled people who cannot or will not work?

9. The Homebound Problem. The more than two million Americans who are so disabled that they cannot regularly leave their homes with the transportation normally available to them for participation in social, educational, or employment activities still are engaged in an uphill struggle to obtain entry into the present federal-state-voluntary agency rehabilitation service structure. Does the future of this group lie primarily in the use of persuasion, pressure, and education to prod the system into opening its doors to them or should a new and more viable system be set up expressly for this group? The National Center for the Rehabilitation of Homebound Persons, at Federation of the Handicapped for one, favors any course of action that will eliminate the social isolation endured by these people. One approach would be a transportation or resettlement model that, to all intents and purposes, eliminates the homebound condition for all but those who cannot under any circumstances leave their homes for community activities. Can homeboundedness be stamped out as a socially induced disability just as polio was defeated as a medical condition?

10. The Learning Problem. The Learning Capacities Project sponsored by the Federation of the Handicapped views rehabilitation primarily as a learning experience for the disabled person. Effective and rapid learning of new behaviors, skills, and ideas is essential if long-term rehabilitation is to occur. Yet, the rehabilitation field is largely insensitive to, and unaware of, the relationship between clients' learning efficiency and rehabilitation workers' instructional activities. Indeed, it has been reported by Rusalem and Rusalem that most rehabilitation failures occur because of the incompatibility between instructional procedures used with a client and the learning style of that client.

Should special regional in-service training programs dealing with a learning capacities approach be funded by government grants and made available to rehabilitation workers throughout the country? Should a national rehabilitation learning capacities center be established to coordinate research and training efforts in this significant new practice?

11. The Disabled Peer Problem. In contrast to the major use of peer and paraprofessional personnel by various programs for alcoholics, drug addicts, and poor persons, the rehabilitation field has made only minor use of such individuals in relation to other disabilities. It may be noted that the rather cautious posture of many rehabilitation professionals in this regard reflects a feeling of insecurity and a lack of trust on the part of top administration. Indeed weak leadership has been provided in clarifying peer roles and practices in rehabilitation. Yet, without attenuating the central professional thrust of the rehabilitation movement, it is possible to successfully use paraprofessionals selectively. For instance, certain disabled persons can provide role models for their contemporaries, while offering encouragement, peer participation, and personal warmth to the rehabilitation client. Obviously, the presence of a disability, experience as a rehabilitation client, and good intentions alone do not automatically qualify a disabled person for a paraprofessional role. However, if the disabled person is properly selected and trained, his contribution to the rehabilitation process could be maximized. Can rehabilitation bridge the gap between improved service opportunities and distrust of paraprofessionals and find ways of integrating peer relationshp practices into the mainstream of the rehabilitation movement?

12. The Age Range Problem. Although no explicit ceiling is set on the age of service applicants, everyday rehabilitation practices often achieve the effect of excluding older clients. This occurs despite conclusive evidence presented by Federation Employment and Guidance Service and other agencies following years of experience that it is altogether economically feasible and professionally rewarding to rehabilitate vocationally-motivated older persons into employment. Similarly, school children, in general, and particularly those in the elementary and preschool subgroups, rarely, if ever, receive the benefits of rehabilitation (as contrasted to special education) services. Has the time come to eliminate all age barriers to effective participation in rehabilitation programs? Should legislation be advocated that assures the rehabilitation and employment rights of older persons? Should rehabilitation be (as with the severely retarded) a lifelong developmental process rather than a finite interval in a person's life that occurs only when an individual is in a particular age range?

13. The Deinstitutionalization Problem. In the current rush to empty institutions of as many intellectually, emotionally, and physically limited persons as possible, officials have paid scant heed to the rehabilitation needs of residents who are about to reenter the community. Since these are severely disabled people with overlays of institutional malaise and isolation, they almost always need protracted periods of preparation for unsheltered or partially sheltered living rather than mere reinsertion into the neighborhood. Should the states mandate that no individual should be released from an institution until he has received adequate rehabilitation services? Should deinstitutionalized persons remain in the community only if they have access to suitable follow-through supports? Should a bill of human rights be set up for institutionalized, about-to-be institutionalized, and formerly institutionalized persons that guarantees them access to the rehabilitation preparation they need for deinstitutionalization?

14. Creative Individual Program Planning. Too many clients are inadequately assessed preparatory to entering a planned rehabilitation program. In some cases, important evaluative components (such as learning capacities) are omitted; in other cases, rehabilitation evaluations are superficial and conducted by inadequately trained personnel who do not possess the complex evaluative skills needed in rehabilitation program planning. In still other cases, limited evaluations are made by a number of practitioners with little organized effort undertaken to synthesize and interrelate the findings. Should we create a network of area diagnostic centers which, without bias and vested interest, can truly assess the complex factors in each case, recommend a program based on these findings, and then, refer the diagnosed person to those community resources which are *best* equipped to deliver the needed service? Too many diagnosed clients are referred for service to agencies that really are not equipped for the task but which meet some irrelevant criterion. Should a rehabilitation diagnostic center offer no other rehabilitation services so as to remove itself from possible conflict of interest in relation to the rehabilitation plan?

15. The Quality Problem. The numbers game in which counselor performance is assessed primarily on the basis of number of successful case closures emphasizes a yardstick that is politically expeditious but rehabilitationally untenable. If individuals and their needs really matter, a quality scoring system for counselor functioning should be instituted. Such a quality system introduces many problems of its own that do not necessarily endear it to rehabilitation administrators. Indeed, a satisfactory quality evaluation program of counselor effectiveness has only recently been started in a few agencies, and it is still too early to judge the outcomes. It is not too early, however, to reward rehabilitation personnel for imaginative, difficult, and challenging case achievements rather than a mere accumulation of closed file folders and meaningless "brownie points."

Undoubtedly, the reader will have priorities that differ from those of the authors. Through discourse, however, we can probably agree in time on a list of outstanding rehabilitation problems that require constructive and innovative solutions. The hopeful element is that persons of goodwill in every rehabilitation stratum want to solve the critical problems of our time in order to improve service to disabled persons. On the other hand, the field has not learned how to use the rare creativity that is in our midst to evolve novel and more effective solutions. Can it be that the central problem of rehabilitation (as in many other fields) is that the power structure is in the hands of those who are not creative thinkers and that they not only cannot generate creativity, but, in some cases, cannot even understand it and cannot bring themselves to use it constructively for the disabled members of our society?